History Plays

PAJ BOOKS

Bonnie Marranca and Gautam Dasgupta

Series Editors

History Plays

CHARLES L. MEE

The Johns Hopkins University Press
Baltimore and London

The Johns Hopkins University Press
2715 North Charles Street, Baltimore, Maryland 21218-4319
The Johns Hopkins Press Ltd., London

Note: War to End War appeared previously in *Theatre Forum* magazine, © 1994
Department of Theatre of the University of California, San Diego; and
The Investigation of the Murder in El Salvador appeared in *Wordplays,* vol. 4 (PAJ),
© 1984 Charles L. Mee., Jr.; *Vienna: Lusthaus* appeared in *Drama Review,* © 1987
New York University and The Massachusetts Institute of Technology; *Orestes*
appeared in *Performing Arts Journal,* © 1993 The Johns Hopkins University Press.

Questions about performance rights for all plays should be addressed to
Sarah Jane Leigh, ICM, 40 West 57th Street, New York, N.Y. 10019.

A catalog record for this book is available from the British Library.

Library of Congress Cataloging-in-Publication Data

Mee, Charles L.
   History plays / Charles L. Mee.
p.   cm. — (PAJ books)
   ISBN 0-8018-5805-4 (alk. paper). — ISBN 0-8018-5792-9
(pbk. : alk. paper)
   1. Historical drama, American.   I. Title.   II. Series.
PS3563.E28H57   1998
812'.54—dc21   97-28922   CIP

Contents

Preface

These plays were composed in the way that Max Ernst made his Fatagaga pieces toward the end of World War I: texts have been taken from, or inspired by, other texts. Among the sources for these pieces are the classical plays of Euripides and texts from the contemporary world.

I think of these appropriated texts as historical documents—as evidence of who and how we are and what we do. And I think of the characters who speak these texts as characters like the rest of us: people through whom the culture speaks, often without the speakers' knowing it.

My work begins with the belief that human beings are, as Aristotle said, social creatures—that we are the product not just of psychology, but also of history and of culture, that we often express our histories and cultures in ways even we are not conscious of, that the culture speaks through us, grabs us and throws us to the ground, cries out, silences us.

I don't write "political" plays in the usual sense of the term, but I write out of the belief that we are creatures of our history and culture and gender and politics—that our beings and actions arise from that complex of influences and forces and motivations, that our lives are richer and more complex than can be reduced to a single source of human motivation.

So I try in my work to get past traditional forms of psychological realism, to bring into the frame of the plays material from history, philosophy, insanity, inattention, distractedness, judicial theory, sudden violent passion, lyricism, the *National Enquirer*, nostalgia, longing, aspiration, literary criticism, anguish, confusion, inability.

I like plays that are not too neat, too finished, too presentable. My plays are broken, jagged, filled with sharp edges, filled with things that take sudden turns, career into each other, smash up, veer off in sickening turns. That feels good to me. It feels like my life. It feels like the world.

And then I like to put this—with some sense of struggle remaining—into a classical form, a Greek form, or a beautiful dance theater piece, or some other effort at civilization.

Vienna: Lusthaus

Vienna: Lusthaus was conceived and directed by Martha Clarke, created with the company of performers, and composed by Richard Peaslee. It had its New York premiere in April 1986, at St. Clement's Episcopal Church and was performed subsequently at the New York Shakespeare Festival, at the Kennedy Center, and in Venice, Vienna, Paris, and elsewhere. It won the Obie for best play in 1986. The text for this piece is taken in part from, or inspired by, Freud, Musil, letters of the Austro-Hungarian imperial family, principles of Viennese architecture, and Diane Wolkstein, among other sources.

Vienna: Lusthaus

Speeches are sometimes identified in the script by the name of the actor who delivered the text. The original cast included Robert Besserer, Brenda Currin, Timothy Doyle, Marie Fourcaut, Lotte Goslar, Robert Langdon-Lloyd, Richard Merrill, Gianfranco Paoluzi, Amy Spencer, Paolo Styron, and Lila York.

At the Cafe (Timothy Doyle and Brenda Currin)

HUGO: I was at a performance of *Fidelio* last night.

MAGDA: At the Hofoper.

HUGO: Yes. I was sitting in the stalls next to Leonard.

MAGDA: Leonard?

HUGO: Kraus's nephew, you know, a man who is, in fact, quite congenial to me.

MAGDA: I'm not sure.

HUGO: A man with whom, in fact, I have long felt I should like to make friends.

MAGDA: Leonard, of course. I understand.

HUGO: At any rate, I was sitting there, quietly enough, inoffensive really, looking at my program, and all of a sudden, without any warning at all, Leonard flew through the air across the seats, put his hand in my mouth, and pulled out two of my teeth.

Aunt Cissi (Timothy Doyle's boudoir speech)

At night Aunt Cissi wore a face mask lined with raw veal.

In strawberry season, she covered her face with crushed fruit.

Always, in every season, she took baths of warm oil to preserve the suppleness of her skin—though once the oil was nearly boiling, and she nearly suffered the fate of a Christian martyr.

She slept on an iron bedstead. She took it with her wherever she went. She slept absolutely flat. She scorned pillows.

Sometimes she slept with wet towels around her waist to keep her figure.

And in the morning she would drink a decoction of egg whites and salt.

Once a month, she had her hair washed with raw egg and brandy. And then she put on a long waterproof silk wrap and walked up and down to dry her hair.

She wore tight-fitting little chemises. And satin and moire corsets made in Paris. She never wore a corset for more than a few weeks before she threw it away.

She wore silk stockings attached to her corset by silk ribbons.

She never wore petticoats. In truth, in the summer, when she took her early morning walks, she would slip her feet into her boots without stockings on, and she wore nothing at all beneath her bodice and skirt, and she would walk forever. She would walk for four or five hours, every day.

She would walk forever and ever.

She could never get enough of walking.

India (Brenda Currin)

I was in India several thousand years ago fondling a horse.

[*Silence. She checks to see if this is going to be believed. Proceeds.*]

A blond-haired boy was on the horse. We were strangers. I was touching the
horse, and then I was touching him, and others were watching us. And then
he came down from the horse and kissed my quim.
Oh . . .
I thought . . .
Oh . . .
He is French, because . . .
because he . . .
because he knew how much I loved to have him . . .
kiss my quim.
And I was very glad. And so we danced.
And I saw that he was very strong, and hard as a rock.
His penis was small, but very firm and round and powerful, and I loved it.
And I was ready to have him come inside me.
But he didn't.
I thought: perhaps this is the way it is in India.
Penetration is not important.
And I felt like a barbarian,
expecting entry
when he had something
more civilized in mind.

Mother's Speech (Brenda Currin)

My mother and I were in a white, sun-filled summer house together, and my
mother was at the top of the stairs, and I was at the bottom looking up at her,
and she said to me all of a sudden: "Do you remember always to hold on to
the bannister when you go up and down stairs?" And I reassured her that I
did, even though I didn't. "Good," she said, and yet, she didn't remember herself, because one day she was carrying an armful of tulips in the upstairs hall-
way, and, even though she had lived in the house for thirty-five years, she
forgot to pay attention, she let her mind wander for a moment, and she
walked right out through an open window and fell to her death.

The Fountain (Robert Langdon-Lloyd)

My daughter and I were standing on a balcony in an interior courtyard looking down at the fountain. She was just about to turn around and go back in to
dance when I said, "No, wait a moment," because I wanted her to see the
fountain. It's beautiful. From the very center comes a great gush of water. Just

at that moment the central plume of water started to rise. It grew higher and higher and I said to Marie, "Perhaps they haven't quite got it under control." And then it inclined slightly toward us so that suddenly the plume of water rose up directly into Marie's face and positively drenched her. And she laughed. I put out my hand to deflect the water so it wouldn't continue to shoot right into her face. And just then a woman's voice called to me from inside the ballroom: "Let her get wet!" "What's that," I said. "Let her get wet," the woman called, "let her get drenched. Otherwise what's the point of life." And so, of course, I did.

Orchard Speech (Timothy Doyle)

I was descending from a great height . . . not the sort of place meant for climbing. I was holding a large branch in my hand that was covered with red blossoms. By the time I got to the bottom the lower blossoms were already a good deal faded. I saw . . . a manservant there. Yes . . . using a piece of wood to comb thick tufts of hair that were hanging from the tree like moss. I asked how I might transplant this beautiful tree into my garden. And this young man put his arm around me and embraced me. I was shocked of course. I pushed him away and asked whether he thought people could just embrace me like that . . . and he said it was allowed.

River Speech (Robert Langdon-Lloyd)

I was standing once on the bank of the Danube near a small bridge with several students from the university. We had gone down to the river with the idea of rowing, and all of us, not just I alone, were struck suddenly by the unexpected beauty of the water, which looked almost silky. We longed to have it run through our fingers, to swim in it, to taste it.

The stream swelled up over the bank, over the wet grass that was a shade of emerald green almost painful in its brilliance and depth. It seemed that the stream overflowed with the very essence of life itself. And then it started to rain. A great, heavy, drenching rain, clear raindrops as large as crystal prisms.

But this was what was most extraordinary of all—it rained on only one half of the river, leaving the other half and its bank in brilliant sunlight. I stood back from it and looked. I couldn't move at all. I understood that I might have stood on this river bank all my life waiting for this to happen—but this would be the only moment that I would be in the midst of such a miracle.

Hugo/Magada (Timothy Doyle and Brenda Currin)
[*speaking both parts together, out of sync*]

I was at a performance of *Fidelio* last night.
At the Hofoper.
Yes. I was sitting in the stalls next to Leonard.
Leonard?
Kraus's nephew, you know, a man who is, in fact, quite congenial to me.
I'm not sure.
A man with whom, in fact, I have long felt I should like to make friends.
Leonard, of course. I understand.
At any rate, I was sitting there, quietly enough, inoffensive really, looking at
my program, and all of a sudden, without any warning at all, Leonard flew
through the air across the seats, put his hand in my mouth, and pulled out
two of my teeth.
Why would he want to do that?
I'm sure I wouldn't know.
Is he a Jew?
No.
So much of life is unaccountable these days.
The other night I was running down the staircase in pursuit of a little girl who
had made some taunting remark to me . . .
Yes.
When, part way down the stairs, an older woman stopped the girl for me so
that I was able to catch up with her.
The little girl.
Yes. Exactly. I can't tell you whether or not I hit her, although I certainly
meant to.
We all have these feelings.
But the most extraordinary thing did happen: the next thing I knew I found
myself copulating with her there in the middle of the staircase, in the mid-
dle of the air as it seemed.
Copulating.
Well, not copulating really; in fact, I was only rubbing my genitals against her
genitals.
This is the little girl still.
Yes, and while I was copulating with her, or, as I said, rubbing my genitals
against her genitals, at the very time I was copulating with her, I saw her genitals extremely distinctly, as well as her head, which was turned upwards and
sideways, if you can imagine just how we were at the time, on the staircase.

No.

Never mind then, but here's the point: while we were copulating like that I noticed hanging above me, to my left, two small paintings—and at the bottom of the smaller of these two paintings, instead of the painter's signature, I saw my own first name. Don't you find that extraordinary?

No.

I Don't Like (Brenda Currin) [*spoken to music*]

I don't like Johann Strauss.
I don't like tropical flowers.
I don't like mother of pearl.
I don't like ivory tortoise shell.
I don't like green silk.
I don't like Venetian glass.
I don't like to have my initials embroidered on the edge of my underwear. All those little songs about love, loneliness, woodland whispers, and twinkling trout.
I don't like crochet.
I don't like tatting.
I don't like antimacassars.
I don't like a house that looks like a pawn shop.
I don't like flower paintings done by archduchesses.
I don't like peacock feathers.
I don't like tarot cards.
I don't like cinnamon in my coffee.
I don't like women who wear a lot of underwear.
I don't like buildings decorated like bits of frosted pastry.
I like my windows without eyebrows.
A man is born in a hospital, dies in a hospital, he ought to live in a place that looks like a hospital.

Sweetgirls: Klara (Robert Langdon-Lloyd)

Klara, a seamstress. Once.
Elke, a shopkeeper's daughter. Twice.
Christine, daughter of a Bohemian weaver. Once. After an evening in the Prater.
Alma, dressmaker. Three times.
Mitzi, an actress. Daughter of a bargeman. Three times.

Lina, a music student. Jew. Once. In the private room at Felix's cafe.
Jeanette, milliner. From Moravia. Five times.
Her friend Elizabeth, a laceworker. Three times.
Grisette, domestic, from the Sudetenland. Once.

Mother's Speech (Brenda Currin)

My mother was sick and she woke up very early one morning in pain. And
she asked the nurse to get her a cup of tea. And as soon as the nurse left the
room, she said: "I'm going to jump out the window with Paulie. Come jump
with us." I said: "Why?" She said: "Because we don't want to live anymore."

Aunt Alexandra (Timothy Doyle)

My Aunt Alexandra, you know, was always convinced that she was covered
with dust, and no one could persuade her otherwise, and so she and her
clothes had always to be brushed by relays of maids and even her food and
drink had to be dusted before her eyes. She believed, too, that a sofa had
become lodged in her head so that she felt it was dangerous for her to try to
go through a door in case she knocked the ends of the sofa.

Black-and-White Butterfly (Timothy Doyle)

This morning, I saw a black-and-white butterfly on a green leaf, and I waved
my hand toward it, and it didn't move. I thought, well, it doesn't notice me.
And then I thought, no; it thinks it is camouflaged. It doesn't realize that its
black-and-white color is the wrong camouflage for a green leaf. It is sitting
there thinking "I am safe," when it is completely exposed. And then I thought,
no; it isn't even thinking whether it is safe or exposed. That whole issue has
been left to natural selection.

The Rat (Robert Langdon-Lloyd)

The other night I returned to the one-room place where I was staying. I
opened the door and saw a gigantic rat.

It looked me right in the eye.

I clapped my hands to frighten it away but it didn't flinch.

So I lunged for it and got it by the neck and started to choke it, gripping tighter and tighter, twisting its neck, but the little bastard wouldn't die . . .

And I thought—This is some kind of Greek Fate, isn't it, to be left forever trying to choke a rat.

The Dead Soldier (Timothy Doyle and Robert Langdon-Lloyd)

SOLDIER: How can you tell when a person's been shot?

SPEAKER: At what hour, you mean?

SOLDIER: No. I mean if they were shot before or after they died. What does *rigor mortis* actually mean?

SPEAKER: That cellular death is complete.

SOLDIER: What does one do to support the lips if the teeth are missing?

SPEAKER: A strip of stiff cardboard, a strip of sandpaper, cotton.

SOLDIER: How does a drowned body look?

SPEAKER: Discoloration over the face, neck, upper chest. Because the body floats downward in the water, usually.

SOLDIER: What colors does a body pass through after death?

SPEAKER: Light pink, red, light blue, dark blue, purple-red.

THE END

The War to End War

The War to End War incorporates texts from Harold Nicolson's memoirs as well as texts by Tristan Tzara, Hans Richter, Kurt Schwitters, Max Ernst, the letters of J. Robert Oppenheimer, and others. It was first produced at Sledgehammer Theatre in San Diego, where it was directed by Matt Wilder.

The War to End War

Characters

NICOLSON
PROUST (VOICE-OVER)
WILSON
CLEMENCEAU
WITTGENSTEIN
DEAD SOLDIERS
AN "ORIENTAL"
AN AFRICAN
BROCKDORFF-RANTZAU

A DANCER
A MAN
ANONYMOUS VOICE-OVER
SCHWITTERS
MONA LISA
OPPENHEIMER (VOICE-OVER)
VON NEUMANN
TELLER
FERMI

I. THE TREATY OF VERSAILLES

The lights go out suddenly with a terrific explosion and a flash of light. Sirens. Explosions. Whistles. Explosive flashes of light. Machine guns. Bottle rockets. Flares. Tons of shattering glass. Dense fog. An operatic aria is heard, or several long, lamenting high notes held by a singer. This all goes on for a very long time. A sickening green light gradually pervades the theater.

As the fog clears, imperceptibly at first, we hear Satie playing one of his nocturnes.

A dozen ornate nineteenth-century chairs are scattered helter-skelter around the stage, and ice buckets with champagne in them, and, at center, a table covered with green baize, not much larger than a card table, with crystal, and a deck of cards.

Gradually, as the fog lifts during this next scene, we see that the entire rear wall is a vast shattered mirror in several large, elaborate, gilt frames—as though a mosaic of broken shards of glass. It is an old mirror, dulled and smoky and incompletely silvered.

To one side is a headless tailor's dummy. Elsewhere, a urinal.

NICOLSON *enters, dressed in morning coat, carrying an umbrella. He sits in one of the chairs, crosses his legs, listens to the Satie nocturne. This time of listening amounts to a musical interlude. Near the end of the Satie piece, Nicolson speaks.*

NICOLSON: We generally meet at ten, there are secretaries behind . . .

PROUST VOICE-OVER [*Whispering*]: Mais non, mais non, vous allez trop vite. Recommencez.

NICOLSON [*After a moment, slowly, exactly*]: The dominant note is: black and white. Heavy black suits, white cuffs and paper. Crucial to get something right I suppose.

[*He takes a glass of champagne from the nearby table.*]

PROUST VOICE-OVER: Précisez, mon cher, précisez.

NICOLSON: Relieved by blue and khaki.

PROUST VOICE-OVER: Vous prenez la voiture de la Délégation. Vous descendez au Quai d'Orsay. Vous montez l'escalier. Vous entrez dans la Salle. Et alors?

NICOLSON [*Sighs, hesitates, resumes.*]: The only other colors would be the scarlet damask of the Quai d'Orsay curtains, green baize. . .

PROUST VOICE-OVER: Précisez, mon cher, précisez.

NICOLSON: pink blotting pads, innumerable gilt of little chairs.

[*Silence*]

For smells you would have petrol, typewriting ribbons, French polish, central heating, a touch of violet hair wash.

[*Silence*]

The tactile motifs would be tracing paper, silk, the leather handle of a weighted pouch of papers, the foot-feel of very thick carpets alternating with parquet floors.

[*Silence*]

What would be the point? What quite had been the point? Of course, there were matters of substance: the structure of the Old World; old empires crumbling; new ones reaching for the spoils; former colonies squirming to stay free; the old order of the Congress of Vienna coming apart; well, and for that matter, Newtonian physics as well; traditional painting; the notion of God—none of it in such good repair really, whether as cause or effect, and then the endless disputes. Matters of honor. Or of interest. Altercations. The assigning of blame. The study of causes. Although, who could say? In time one became more inclined to see systemic features—the eternal business of those who had the power and those who wanted it. One had entered a logic trap. One needed an epiphany to escape. One became a sleepwalker, like all the others.

[*A cello solo*]

PROUST VOICE-OVER: Précisez, mon cher, précisez.

NICOLSON: Yes, well: we met. The stretch of muscle caught by leaning constantly over very large maps, the brittle feel of a cane chair seat which had been occupied for hours. These things seemed to matter a great deal. That sort of thing. A sense of hopelessness. Of dread. Of knowing one had no intention of doing anything real.

[*Projected through the partly silvered mirror, from the rear, a pencil-thin red line is slowly drawn. It takes several minutes for the line to be completed, and, at the end, it is labeled with its date, 78 B.C. During the next twenty minutes, one after another red line is slowly drawn, and each one labeled with its date—the ever-changing borders of Germany for the past 2000 years.*]

PROUST VOICE-OVER: N'allez pas trop vite.

NICOLSON: A group of little men at the end of a vast table: maps, interpreters, secretaries, and row upon row of empty gilt chairs. The great red curtains are drawn, scarlet and enclosing against the twilight sinking gently upon the Seine.

PROUST VOICE-OVER [*Almost entirely inaudible now*]: Précisez . . .

NICOLSON: Tea, brioches, macaroons, the tea-urn guttering in the draught. Reassuring rituals. Messieurs, nous avons donc examiné la frontière entre Csepany et Saros Patag. . . . Il résulte que la jonction du chemin de fer

Miskovec-Kaschau avec la ligne St. Peter-Losoncz doit être attribuée. . . Ah, these interminable struggles. . . the infinite langour of the minister slowly uncrossing his knees, the crackle of Rolls Royces on the gravel of the courtyard. . . Wir wissen das die Gewalt der deutschen. Waffen begrochen ist. Wir kennen die Macht des Hasses, die uns hier.

[*As he speaks,* CLEMENCEAU *enters, helped in by an African in a burnoose and an Asian in a chef's hat. Clemenceau wears grey gloves, holds one hand to his heart, where he has been shot, and is bleeding. He sits, finally, after a long entrance, with the elaborate assistance of the African and the Asian, exhausted, and coughs, his lungs filled with blood.*]

At the end one walked over the fields. At Verdun the shallow graves were being washed out by the rain. Feet stuck up out of the ground, and helmets with skulls in them rose up out of the mud. At Belleau Wood one saw great crater holes, splintered trees, shards of farmhouses through the white mist, shrapnel embedded in the woods, and nothing else, no grass, nothing, only a fine powder covering all, and there, amidst the wilderness of shell holes, one was in danger of getting lost; there was no sign of direction. What few ruins there were reminded one of antiquity. Indeed from Rheims all the way to Soissons one had the impression of having passed out of the modern world back into a vanished civilization.

[WILSON *enters. He wears pince-nez, high starched collar, is sick and weak, has difficulty breathing, is helped in by a dead soldier, who wears white gloves, has a white bandage around his head, perhaps carries a bouquet of flowers, and is extremely pale. A long entrance, till Wilson is helped to lie down on a chaise.*]

Here there was utter desolation, dead trenches, white chalky parapets, barbed wire, and silence. No living thing, no bird, no animal broke the silence. Death white this landscape was, death white. And when I returned to my hotel and gave my clothes to the chambermaid to have them cleaned, I remarked to her that the white mud would be hard to get out, that it was the dust of Verdun. And she took the clothes reverently and with a tone I shall never forget she said, "Yes, that is very precious dust, sir."

[*Enormously sad music fills the theater. A dreamy stillness on stage.* CLEMENCEAU *coughs.* NICOLSON *sits silently, in thought. All turn to see that* BROCKDORFF-RANTZAU *has just entered. He is escorted by* WITTGENSTEIN, *dressed in prison stripes. He holds hat in hand, has rimless eyeglasses, dueling scar on cheek. Wittgenstein helps Brockdorff-Rantzau to a chair, steps back. Brockdorff-Rantzau sits silently throughout, hat and briefcase in his lap. Shriveled. Gradually, during the course of the scene, everyone except Brockdorff-Rantzau will end up holding a champagne glass and drinking from it. Gradually, too, during the course of the scene, several trapdoors will open in the stage, and bodies will rise up out of their graves and ascend to heaven—very slowly; the ascensions will take the whole of this first section to complete. Shortly after the bodies have begun to ascend, and equally slowly, four lucite boxes, like the box in which Eichmann sat for his trial, will begin to descend. Eventually, they will descend onto, and cover, Clemenceau, Wilson, Nicolson, and Brockdorff-Rantzau.]*

WILSON [*Speaking deliberately, pausing often to allow time for his words to be heard.*]: I am the sort of person, I must admit, who likes the same sweater, for instance, the same automobile ride, the same woman. In fact, nothing pleases me more than taking an automobile ride along a familiar route wearing the sweater I wore in my Princeton days. Think of it. You know. Poetry. The same passages from the same books. Old college songs. The good things, the simple pleasures I suppose. We might all agree. Nothing extravagant. When I take a vacation I go to the same place every time, the lake country in England, and ride my bicycle over the hills. I'm fond of England, Europe generally. Europe as a whole. Exceptions here and there, of course, who wouldn't have? But on the whole, you know. And even so, one must admit, sometimes, of the possibility of the new.

CLEMENCEAU [*To Wittgenstein*]: Here. You're a man interested in language.

WITTGENSTEIN: Yes . . .

CLEMENCEAU: Of course you are. Now, where do you suppose the word bugger comes from?

WITTGENSTEIN: Well . . .

CLEMENCEAU: You wouldn't know. Of course you wouldn't know, but take a guess. You couldn't guess. All right, then, I'll tell you. Bulgaria! It comes from Bulgaria, where all they did, so I've been told, was bugger each other for three or four centuries. It was their religion, they said. They thought the world such a horrible place that they refused to bring more children into it. Did you know that? And so they buggered each other for centuries! What do you think, was this an admirable thing to do? These German hordes bugger you up the backside and fuck you in the mouth at the same time, bash your skull in when they've finished, and tell you it's their religion. That's how I understand the story. Nice people.

[*Coughs*]

Some people are like this. Take it as a given, that's all. Next thing you know they're at your front and your back. That's how it is with these people. Part of the splendid variety of human nature. I make no moral judgment. But I've never seen a good German, you can be sure of that—outside a concert hall.

[*Coughs*]

Bad enough when you get two of them together. Everything is more than doubled. It's always geometric with these bastards. Think of Beethoven.

[*Coughs*]

DEAD SOLDIER: When the politicians think, even the rats have to vomit.

CLEMENCEAU: I spoke to Billy Hughes last night. I said to him, all right Billy, if we give you fellows the mandate for New Guinea, will you give your word the natives will have access to the missionaries? Oh, yes, I would indeed, sir, he said, for there are many days when these poor devils do not get half enough missionaries to eat!

[*Laughs and coughs*]

Not half enough missionaries to eat! There's a rich story if you let it fill your mind!

[*Coughs*]

Every man a bloody axe in his hand, eh?

"ORIENTAL": Every act is a pistol shot!

DEAD SOLDIER: It's the worst bastards that rise to the top in this world.

WILSON: Well, let's hope not!

CLEMENCEAU: A woman came to me the other day, English woman, nice woman, wanted to do something, she said, wanted to work in the hospitals. OK, I said. Good enough. Gave her a job taking care of the Montenegrins, and what do you suppose she found? Next to this one fellow's bed, a leather bag, big leather bag. She opened it up, and there inside this fine English woman found sixty human noses. Not fake noses. Real human noses. Nice fellows these Montenegrins. Of course one wishes there weren't any Montenegrins in the world!

WILSON: And even so. . .

CLEMENCEAU: I've had a gut full of niceties, I can tell you that.

WILSON: Yet, nonetheless . . .

CLEMENENCEAU: Now you see it: the English sent their missionaries on ahead; the Americans send their liberals.

"ORIENTAL": Man knows no more about life than the stink mushroom does, when you come down to it.

WITTGENSTEIN: I wouldn't know. I don't read the papers.

CLEMENCEAU [*Addressing Brockdorff-Rantzau, shouting*]: When I was a boy, what do you think my father did? In Nantes. Took me one day to the reading room, where people came to read and gossip, old people, people who had seen the Revolution and Napoleon. Over there, he said. Do you see that fellow over there? An old friend of Marat. Marat! That's how close we are to those days. Well, sure, I wasn't very clear who this Marat was or what he had done, but Marat was a tremendous name. All that blood, you know, the Revolution, Charlotte Corday, the bathtub full of blood. I had great respect for that old cocker who had known Marat. You can't escape history. It holds you in its fist. Here's this fellow who goes back to 1789! Then there was the year of the Paris Commune: 1870. When the Germans came onto French soil. I was there. That's how far back I myself go. 1870! Extraordinary when you think of it. The past reaches over the years to keep its grip on you. These Americans! Think they can simply step to another planet! Who wouldn't want to? Does a man like to be held eternally by the scruff of the neck?

[*To Nicolson*]

And then some of these fellows want something, don't they? You wouldn't know, of course, but what do you think? No, really, you don't know. To be sure, you don't think! And so you see nothing! You express your anguish, you speak of ideals, you lament the loss, but in truth, given the chance, you wouldn't do a thing about it. You'd express your compassion, hand out a few bits of charity, even bribes, but you wouldn't change a thing when it came down to it. You'd pick up your gun to keep hold of what you've got. Because there's something you want as well! You've got it in your fist. Or got some poor bastard to hold it for you so you can rail against him while he keeps a safe hold on it for you. I've had a gut full of hypocrites as well, I can tell you. And then we have to sit here and listen to your misgivings! I believe in saints. I am not a man entirely without belief. I should have been a saint myself, I have a talent for it, a taste for it, a longing for it, but instead I've spent my life among men like you.

[*He ends in a paroxysm of coughing, which continues for a few minutes through the following dialogue.*]

DEAD SOLDIER: We motored out to Fontaine-aux-Charmes yesterday, with Riddell and Balfour. Extraordinary place. The ravines. Old helmets. Rusted firearms. Old boots.

WILSON: Is this relevant?

DEAD SOLDIER: Back where the lines had been drawn over the maps and charts nothing could resist the forward progress of the generals' pencils: no bogs, no gas. No stink of blood and latrine to spoil the odor of optimism.

WILSON: Is this going to be relevant?

DEAD SOLDIER: No punctured stomachs of dead men to release that distinctive odor. No sounds of snoring and groans from men whose helmets had been blown off their heads, helmets splashed with brain.

WILSON: I think we know all this.

DEAD SOLDIER: Legs blown up against their backs.

NICOLSON: I think we could move along to another topic now.

DEAD SOLDIER: No men going mad from lack of air.

WILSON: No point in stirring up old hatreds.

CLEMENCEAU: Let him go on! These are Frenchmen he speaks of!

DEAD SOLDIER: At Grurie Wood, I hear, a Captain Juge, standing upright on his parapet, revolver in his hand, cheering on his men, fell, wounded, rose to his feet again, calling to his men, "Stand your ground, stand your ground, stand your ground and be brave," and then, wounded once again, fell again and got up once more, firing point blank at the enemy, who shot him again. Two companies came to his aid, and they came under attack, too, this time from the rear, and when they ran out of ammunition, they retreated through the trenches a yard at a time, fighting hand to hand, building barricades behind them as they went, until at last, they fought off the Germans with their bayonets and the butt ends of their rifles, and the captain called out, "Forward!" and nobody replied, and he rose to his feet one more time and called out: "You bloody cowards! Are you leaving me to go on alone then?" And his platoon sergeant, lying in the trench with a broken shoulder, answered back to him: "Not cowards, sir! Willing enough. But all fucking dead!"

CLEMENCEAU [*Weeping*]: God bless them! God bless these boys!

NICOLSON: Clearly these are Englishmen he speaks of, not French.

WILSON: Yes, well, nonetheless . . .

NICOLSON: This is nothing new.

WILSON: My father used to say emotion is not a political passion.

NICOLSON: One doesn't want to have one's reason swayed by such things.

DEAD SOLDIER: And then one hears of the riots for shoes.

WITTGENSTEIN: People in the streets.

DEAD SOLDIERS: Bodies, too.

WITTGENSTEIN: The need for more police.

WILSON: There is a certain natural terror, of course, of things coming up from the bottom.

AFRICAN: As in feces, I suppose.

DEAD SOLDIER: Or Africans.

WITTGENSTEIN: Vomit.

NICOLSON: Australians, for that matter.

"ORIENTAL": The dark side.

WITTGENSTEIN: One hears about it in mythology.

WILSON: One need not go into it.

NICOLSON: It is a natural reaction, really. Until these people are ready. As in bad news, or passions, certain hatreds, rages, the demons of old, evil forces, psychological sorts of things, you know, all these things, not bad to keep down, until the conscious mind is quite ready to cope with it, you know.

AFRICAN: Given time, one supposes.

DEAD SOLDIER: If ever.

AFRICAN: There's the trick.

NICOLSON: Or else, very well, then, certainly you can turn it loose. Winnie, you know, thinks we ought simply to turn the armies around and sick them on the Bolshies. Keep the Germans in place, there's his idea; keep them armed, turn them around, join them together with the British and the Americans, and keep right on marching to Moscow! How would you like that, then?

WITTGENSTEIN: Not a wholly bad idea.

NICOLSON: But really, what right have you?

AFRICAN: In former times, statesmen never spoke of rights.

NICOLSON: In former times they spoke of nothing else.

WITTGENSTEIN: In former times, statesmen went around looking quite solemn, but that's a thing of the past I think. These days even soldiers and sailors are seen smiling.

DEAD SOLDIER: This is the age of the smile, I think.

WILSON: Of course, one would like to make it good.

NICOLSON: One doesn't like to feel as though one is simply thrown into the middle of a riot in a parrot house.

WITTGENSTEIN: One doesn't like to improvise with the world.

NICOLSON: One doesn't like to think one chooses a king for Albania simply because he dresses in kilts like the Scots.

AFRICAN: Although, personally, I should rather be the Duke of Atholl than King of Albania.

NICOLSON: Or that one will simply be feeding missionaries to the cannibals.

WILSON: Or that we sent these boys to die in vain.

NICOLSON: Or that one can't even number the pages.

AFRICAN: I don't quite take your point.

WILSON: It seems one could get on with it. Surely reasonable men could agree.

CLEMENCEAU: I think of my old friend Baber, of India. Had a pile of heads brought to him every morning. And when the pile was smaller than usual, he would say:"It's pretty small, this pile. My men are getting slack."

BROCKDORFF-RANTZAU: Of course, one doesn't want to leave one's children. One tries as best one can to sort it out, but the mind is a finite thing. We are wise enough to know that our antidogmatism is as exclusivist as a bureaucrat, that we are not free yet shout freedom, if you see what I mean. A harsh necessity without discipline or morality and we spit on humanity. We are circus directors whistling amid the winds of carnivals convents bawdy houses theaters realities sentiments restaurants, if nothing is lost in the translation. Imagine! That one might learn nothing from such an appalling misadventure!

Well, we know the earth is not a fresh-air resort. Nature does not run along the little thread on which reason would like to see it run. We can of course insure our house against fire our cash register against burglary or our daughter against devirgination, but heaven looks nevertheless down into the bottomless pots of our home countries and extracts the sweat of fear from our foreheads. From out of every plank seat a black claw grabs us by the backside. Like water off the duck's back so love runs off the human bacon. In loneliness man rides down the Styx on his chamber pot. Water fire earth air have been gnawed at by man. No hallelujah can help him. There is no further mention that man the measure of all things gets away with a black eye. Einstein gives man a good drubbing and sends him home. Gives him a good drubbing and sends him home!

With staring eyes and mug hanging wide open this landscape roars through the void, only a handful of snuff remains of the Sphinx, the Olympus, and Louis XV; the Golden Rule and other valuable rules have vanished without leaving a trace, a chair leg clings sea-sick with madness to a torture stake. People have not yet succeeded in unveiling the world through reason! A great deal in the new doctrine does not fit together like a meander in patent leather shoes who goes walking on the arm of a somnambulist box of sardines through the sooty *hortus deliciarum*, if you see what I mean. Einstein does not want to cover up the asphodel meadows. Einstein's poems have nothing to do with modern alarm clocks. Before them reason takes its tail between its legs and goes philandering somewhere else. Yes yes yes the earth is not a valley of tears in the breast pocket!

[*Silence*]

AFRICAN: Are they at an impasse then?

"ORIENTAL": And yet life goes on.

AFRICAN: You see what's come of it.

WITTGENSTEIN: Indeed, the cows sit on top of telegraph poles.

[*The dialogue moves with dizzying speed.*]

DEAD SOLDIER: Tornadoes whirl around in my mouth.

WITTGENSTEIN: If such a thing is possible.

DEAD SOLDIER: Hurricanes.

WITTGENSTEIN: If such a thing is possible.

DEAD SOLDIER: Yes.

WITTGENSTEIN: Bring color to my lips.

DEAD SOLDIER: The marvellous is always beautiful.

AFRICAN: Anything marvellous is beautiful.

DEAD SOLDIER: In fact, only the marvellous is beautiful.

WITTGENSTEIN: Well said, I thought, even though one is of course bored by speeches. And then one speculates: did he speak well? Did he speak well enough? Will it be a remembered speech? Could it have been improved? Did he believe it himself?

AFRICAN: Doesn't his wife look like hell in orchids?

WITTGENSTEIN: Impressions count.

AFRICAN: The power of words.

WITTGENSTEIN: And pictures.

"ORIENTAL": The logic of death.

DEAD SOLDIER: Rather than the cold. The lack of food.

WITTGENSTEIN: Of animal fats, primarily.

DEAD SOLDIER: The sallow complexions.

NICOLSON: Well, make no mistake: civilization requires a little repression. But is the present arrangement such a dreadful thing? Let us imagine, for example, that everyone were suddenly able to afford the same shoes and restaurants, then how would they distinguish themselves from one another? By degrees of intelligence perhaps. Is this any more fair? Indeed, it may be far more desperate. For one can never change the brains one is born with, but one can always change the amount of money in one's bank account. I don't say it always happens, no. But when you consider how really pernicious it could become. Or consider a theocracy, where those who are the purest of heart are at the top. And everyone's heart is presumably subject to investigation to see just how pure it is. Only in heaven is there no repression. Or in hell. Here on earth, we repress one another all the time, and I for one favor it! If one were to say, let A equal a bit of repression, then let B equal death, then, if not A then B you see what I mean.

WITTGENSTEIN: Or, on the other hand, if A then B.

NICOLSON: How's that?

WITTGENSTEIN: Equally logical.

NICOLSON: It's a different syllogism.

WITTGENSTEIN: It may be.

NICOLSON: Not my syllogism.

WITTGENSTEIN: But, do you like it?

AFRICAN: I like it.

WITTGENSTEIN: One tries to be reasonable.

AFRICAN: There is a train of thought. A sort of logic.

"ORIENTAL": That has its own elegance.

WITTGENSTEIN: And momentum, often times.

AFRICAN: It will reach its conclusion.

WITTGENSTEIN: And where does it lead?

DEAD SOLDIER: On the other hand, one might say: if the conclusion is absurd, then the process of reasoning is faulty.

AFRICAN: That would be something else.

DEAD SOLDIER: Another way of saying it.

AFRICAN: Or another way of saying something else.

WITTGENSTEIN: Well, one goes to logical conclusions.

AFRICAN: If one can.

WITTGENSTEIN: So one fears.

AFRICAN: And yet, if you want to get down to earth, do you have gold faucets?

WITTGENSTEIN: What's that?

AFRICAN: In your bathroom. Here.

WITTGENSTEIN: I suppose I do, yes.

AFRICAN: Aren't you afraid for them?

WITTGENSTEIN: How's that?

AFRICAN: Aren't you afraid the servants might get them?

NICOLSON: I should think the faucets are bolted in.

AFRICAN: Are they?

NICOLSON: Well, I'm not a plumber, but I should think one bolts them in, somehow.

AFRICAN: My commode has disappeared.

NICOLSON: The commode is disappearing all over Europe, I think.

WILSON: There are too many committees.

CLEMENCEAU: Indeed.

[*Silence*]

I didn't know.

WITTGENSTEIN: And the dinners.

NICOLSON: The opera with Paderewski.

WILSON: I had a vision of myself this morning: I saw myself under a white sheet; with just my feet sticking out at the bottom, as though I were a body.

CLEMENCEAU: Dead.

WILSON: Yes. I thought: what have I done?

CLEMENCEAU: What did you mean to do?

WILSON: One hopes to do something! And then one finds that time has passed!

NICOLSON: Sometimes one has the feeling one has simply outlived one's time. All sorts of things have been set loose, after all. And why not? These Burmese chaps, for instance. Arabians. It won't be easy to get them back in the bottle, will it?

DEAD SOLDIER: Women.

WITTGENSTEIN: In what context?

DEAD SOLDIER: Let loose.

WITTGENSTEIN: Really?

DEAD SOLDIER: You don't think so?

WITTGENSTEIN: Oh, quite possibly. Sexuality of all kinds, really, I suppose.

DEAD SOLDIER: What do you like in a woman?

WITTGENSTEIN: I hadn't thought about it, really.

DEAD SOLDIER: I like a woman who cries out and sings.

WITTGENSTEIN: Yes. Indeed.

DEAD SOLDIER: I like a slippery woman.

WITTGENSTEIN: Oh, to be sure.

DEAD SOLDIER: I like a woman like a tuba.

WITTGENSTEIN: Ah-ha, yes.

"ORIENTAL": I like a woman with a small boy.

DEAD SOLDIER: I like a woman big with child.

WITTGENSTEIN: I like a woman who's not afraid to jump from a hot air balloon.

NICOLSON: I like a woman's buttocks in a mirror.

[*All look at him.*]

DEAD SOLDIER: Really?

WITTGENSTEIN: And all these throat germs, you know. There are throat germs everywhere. And assassinations as well.

AFRICAN: Perhaps it's not all bad then, when you come to think of it.

NICOLSON: At dinner at the countess's the other night, there were a hundred guests, and a tenor sang in the courtyard below: dirges and laments, all unspeakably moving. Everyone cried. I did myself. And then the countess announced that some people would have to die. Well, the effect was quite extraordinary. Some of the guests ran from the dining room. Balfour took one of the servant's bicycles and rode away. And then a Montenegrin chap took a butcher's knife and held it to the countess's throat and announced to everyone that she was dead. But the countess got very angry at that and refused to be dead. And then everyone was quite put out with her: after all, hadn't she set the rules?

Although one can become too overwrought about these things, I find. Think about it, you know: for all we know there have been other quite advanced civilizations on earth before, possibly more advanced even than our own. If they flourished before the Ice Age, for instance, there is no reason to think they would have left a trace behind. By now even their pottery would be dust. If we vanish, for instance, in fifteen or twenty thousand years there will be no physical evidence left at all of our ever having been here: we have nothing that lasts nearly as long as red pottery.

CLEMENCEAU: Is there at least some entertainment?

[*A* DANCER *runs in at full speed, stops as though caught suddenly in the headlights of a car, frozen, frightened. The "music" that accompanies her is composed of occasional abrupt sounds of breaking glass, rifle fire, machine guns, collapsing buildings, and so forth. She wears long, flowing Greek robes. She moves through various postures, freezing in each one, then whirling to the next. The politicians watch, as though at a concert performance. Occasional bursts of applause come over the loudspeakers. At the end the* DANCER *turns and runs out at full speed. The "music" continues.*

CLEMENCEAU, WILSON, *and* NICOLSON *descend through trapdoors, and their boxes rise quickly into the flies.* BROCKDORFF-RANTZAU *remains on stage, and his box rises quickly into the flies. He sits silently.*]

II. DADA

[*An explosion of popular 1920s German music. A rusted steel wall is slowly lowered to cover the shattered mirror.*

   It can be said that the play begins here—a large choreographed piece, played against the dialogue, with the dialogue serving as music or setting for the choreography of actors running, throwing one another into the steel wall, and so forth. What has preceded can be considered the prologue; what follows this section can be considered the epilogue.

   A MAN *runs in circles, round and round, occasionally tripping, looking around to see what has tripped him, continuing to run, finally tripping and fall-ing repeatedly.*]

VOICE-OVER: Ah yes Sonya, they all take the celluloid doll for a changeling and shout: God save the King!

[*Canned laughter*]

The whole Monist club is gathered on the steamship Meyerbeer. But only the pilot has any conception of high C.

[*Canned laughter*]

I pull the anatomical atlas out of my toe; a serious study begins. Have you seen the fish that have been standing in front of the opera in cutaways for the last two days and nights?

[*Canned laughter. Catcalls, whistles, sirens.*]

Ah ah ye great devils—ah ah ye keepers of the bees and commandants. With a bow wow wow with a boe woe woe, who today does not know what our Father Homer wrote I hold my peace and war in my toga but today I'll take a cherry flip.

[*Canned laughter. Sounds of airplane engines starting.* WITTGENSTEIN *comes out very slowly and solemnly, slowly and ceremoniously strips naked, then turns his backside to the audience, moons them for a while, and then finally makes his buttocks jump up and down as though in time to music.*]

Today nobody knows whether he was tomorrow. They beat time with a coffin lid. And fuck the politicians.

[*Canned laughter*]

I say fuck the politicians.

[*Canned laughter*]

I say fuck the politicians.

[*Canned laughter*]

If you get my meaning.

[*Uproarious canned laughter*]

If only somebody had the nerve to rip the tail feathers out of the trolley car it's a great age.

[*Canned laughter*]

I say, if this is political philosophy, give me a chocolate egg cream.

[*Hilarious canned laughter. More airplane engines. Other engines. The sounds of heavy equipment. Garage doors opening. Clanking. While this voice-over continues with the dialogue below, another is added to it, that of Kurt Schwitters, so that we hear two voices over the loudspeakers at once. Schwitters is calm, but insistent.*
  Continuing throughout: the sounds of cowbells, farting, pot covers banging, rattles, whistles, crashing glasses, a wailing woman, a moaning woman crying for help or sympathy, hiccups, a yodeling woman, canned laughter.]

SCHWITTERS: Take gigantic surfaces, conceived as infinite, cloak them in color, shift them menacingly. Let points burst like stars among them. Let a line rush by. Take a dentist's drill, a meat grinder, a car-track scraper, take buses and pleasure cars, bicycles, tandems and their tires. Make locomotives crash into one another. Explode steam boilers. Take petticoats and other kindred articles, shoes and false hair, also ice skates and throw them into place where they belong. Take man-traps, automatic pistols, infernal machines, the tinfish and the funnel. Inner tubes are highly recommended. Even people can be used. People can even be tied to backdrops. Now marry the oilcloth to the homeowner's loan association, bring the lamp cleaner together with the marriage between Anna Blume and A-natural, concert pitch. Give the globe to the surface to gobble up and you cause a cracked angle to be destroyed by the beam of a twenty-two thousand–candle power arc lamp. Make a human walk on his hands and wear a hat on her feet. Organs backstage sing and say: "Futt, futt." The sewing machine rattles along in the lead. A man in the wings says, "Bah!" Drums and flutes flash death and a streetcar conductor's whistle gleams bright. A melody of violins shimmers pure and virgin-tender. A soft rustling. Even the sewing machine is dark.

[*The* AFRICAN *runs through at top speed, grabs Wittgenstein and propels him off the stage. A few moments later,* WITTGENSTEIN *runs through with the African in his grip and propels him off the other side. They repeat this back and forth.*]

VOICE-OVER [*Continuing*]: The professors of zoology gather in the meadows. With the palms of their hands they turn back the rainbow.

[*Mona Lisa enters, naked, with a mustache, puts her arms out to her sides and turns around and around.*]

MONA LISA: OOOOOOOOOOOOOOOO
OOOOOOOOOOOOOOOOOOOOO
OOOOOOOOOOOOOOOOO
OOOOOOOOO OOOO
OOOOOOOOOOOOOOOO OOOO
O

VOICE-OVER [*Continuing*]: Then typhoons if such a thing is possible. Hurricanes if such a thing is possible

[*The beginning of a long slow siren that builds steadily. Flashing red light as though on top of a police car.*]

VOICE-OVER: cry my voice. Cry my name.

[*Canned laughter*]

Human flesh pulsates at my call. Parrots falling from the branches. The rivers beneath the bridge of sighs. High hats of tin. Tents pitched from morning to night. A great slaughter fills you out.

[*The clanking of steel, as though large steel pieces are being put into place to build a tower. Also echoing corridors, heels against steel.*]

BROCKDORFF-RANTZAU [*His voice miked, speaking quietly*]: eure Adern sind blau rot grun und orangefarben wie die Gesichte der Ahnen die im Sonntagsanzuge am Bord der Altare hocken Zylinderhüte riesige o aus Zinn und Messing machen ein himmlisches Konzert

[*The sounds of destruction, but very distant.*]

die Gestalten der Engel schweben um eueren Ausgang als der Widerschein giftiger Blüten so formet ihr euere Glieder über den Horizont hinaus in den Kaskaden von seinem Schlafsofa stieg das indianische Meer die Ohren voll Watte gesteckt.

VOICE-OVER [*A message, as though broadcast into air-raid shelters in an alert, but spoken by a bored voice*]: Rouge bleu rouge bleu rouge bleu rouge bleu rouge bleu rouge bleu rouge bleu rouge bleu rouge bleu rouge bleu rouge bleu rouge bleu rouge bleu rouge bleu rouge bleu rouge bleu

[*A dog barks, over and over.*]

MONA LISA:
OOOOOOOOOOOOOOOOOOOOOOOOOOOOOOOOOOOOOO
OOOOOOOOOOOO OOOOOOOOOOO
OOOO OOO

DEAD SOLDIER: Boum boum boum
il deshabilla   sa chair quand les   grenouilles
humides commancerent   à bruler   j'ai   mis
le cheval   dans l'âme   du serpent   à Bucarest on dépendra
      mes amis
dorénavant et c'est   très   intéressant.

SCHWITTERS [*Entering, glass held in hand as though for a toast, speaks simultaneously with the others.*]: My friends, after the many excellent speeches here tonight I feel the urge to thank the great, courageous, high-spirited people of Berlin and especially the officers who are here with us this evening. I shall recite my poem, "The raid on Adrianople."

Adrianople est cerné de toutes parts
SSSSSrrrrr zitzitzitzit PAAAAAAAA AAAAAAAAghrrrrrrrrrrrrrr
Ouah ouah ouah, départ des trains suicides,
ouah, ouah, ouah
Tchip tchip tchip—Feeeeeeeeeeee eeeeeeeeeeeeeee eeeelez!

[*He whirls and smashes a wine glass against the back wall.*]

Tchip tchip tchip—des messages télégraphiques, couturières Américaines
Piiiiiiiiiiiiing, sssssssssssssrrrrrrrrrrrr, zitzitzitzit, toum toum Patrouille tapie—

[*He throws himself on top of the table.*]

Vaniteeeeee, viande congeléeeeeee—veilleuse de La Madone.

[*He ends on a whispering note, and then slowly slides to the floor, pulling the green baize cloth with him, along with whatever plates and glasses and silverware are on the table. He lies, as though dead, the green baize pulled over him.*]

WITTGENSTEIN [*Twirling around and around, his arms out to his sides, and then turning and running full tilt into the steel wall, which is miked to resound when he hits it, falling, getting up again, repeating the same.*]:
rrrrrrrrrrrrrrrrrrr   rrrrrrrr
rrrrrr   rrrrrrrrrrrrrrrrrrrrrrrrrrrrrrr
rr   rrrrrrr   rrrrrrrrrrrrrrr
rrrrrrrrrrrrrrrrrrrrrrrrrrrrrrrrrrrrr   rrrr
rrrrrr   rrrrrrrrrrr   rrrrrrrrrrrrrrrrr

AFRICAN: Where the honeysuckle vine twines itself around the door a sweetheart mine is waiting patiently for me can hear the weopur will arrrrrrrrr-rround arrrrrrround the hill

DEAD SOLDIER: les griffes   des morsures
équatoriales
Dimanche deux   éléphants *Journal de*   *Genève*
au restaurant   Le télégraphiste assassiné

AFRICAN: my great room is mine admirabily
comfortably Grandmother said

MONA LISA: OOOOOOOOOOOOOOOOOOOO
OOOOOOOO   OOOOOOOOOOOOOOO
O   OOO   OOOOOO
OOOOOOOOOOOOOOOOO   OOO

WITTGENSTEIN: rrrrrrrrrr
      rrrrrrrrrrrrrrr rrrrrrrrrrrrrr

VOICE-OVER: rouge bleu   rouge bleu
rouge bleu   rouge bleu

AFRICAN: I love the ladies I love the ladies I love to be among the girls And when it's five o'clock and tea is set I like to have my tea with some brunette

MONA LISA: Everybody's doing it, doing it, doing it, everybody's doing it, doing it, doing it

[*The singing continues while Brockdorff-Rantzau speaks.*]

BROCKDORFF-RANTZAU: Aus den gefleckten Tuben strömen die Flusse in die Schatten der legendigen Bäume

Papageien und Assgeier fallen von den Zweigen immer auf den Grund

Bastmatten sind die Wände des Himmels und aus den Wolken kommen die grossen Fallschirme der Magier Larven von Wolkenhaut haben sich die Türme vor die blendenden Augen gebunden

O ihr Flüsse Unter derponte dei sospiri fanget ihr auf Lungen und Lebern und abgeschnittene Hälse

In der Hudsonbay aber flog die Sirene oder ein Vogel Greif oder ein Menschenweibchen von neuestem Typus mir eurer Hand greift ihr in die Taschen der Regierungsräte die voll sind von Pensionen allerhand gutem Willen und schönen Leberwürsten was haben wir alles getan vor euch wie haben wir alle gebetet vom Skorpionstich schwillet der Hintern den heiligen

Sängern und Ben Abka der Hohepriester wälzt sich im Mist

DEAD SOLDIER [*Singing*]: See that ragtime couple over there, see her throw her shoulders in the air. She said to him as she raised her heart oh yes oh yes oh yes oh yes yes yes yes oh yes oh yes oh yes oh yes oh yes oh yes yes yes yes yes oh yes. Sir.

[*The* DEAD SOLDIER *repeats this speech.*]

[*Full volume thundering music frantic, with a strong beat. Deafening. Perhaps something by Einsturzende Neubauten or Cabaret Voltaire.*
    A Rube Goldberg contraption of enormous complexity and stupidity slowly descends, deus ex machina fashion, from above. Swelling heavenly music under]

the music of Einsturzende Neubauten. THE ACTORS *stand amazed. One kneels. One prostrates himself entirely. The contraption blinks its lights. At last it lands on the stage. The music continues, crashing, filled with the sounds of trucks starting, clanking, voices of airplane pilots, static.*

WITTGENSTEIN *steps up to it, takes out a cigar. The contraption whirls, cranks, flails, rocks, and finally produces a light for Wittgenstein's cigar.* THE ACTORS *all pause a moment silently, then all turn and run out at top speed, and the contraption explodes with a huge ball of fire and enormous smoke and ascends into the flies. The music ends with clanking, echoing banging against steel walls, hoarse crying out and wailing in the night.*]

III. LOS ALAMOS (co-written with Mark Murphy Scott)

[*A silver screen descends to cover the shattered mirror. The nineteenth-century chairs are replaced by silver chairs. A vision of the technological future.*

There are occasional zinging sounds, as of a laser, or an electron in an acceleration chamber. Space sounds. The stage is bathed in beautiful shades of red, including pink and coral. Projections of bubble chamber tracks. Throughout the scene we see dreamy, silent projections—as though on a large green television screen—of the precise course, like trails of little white bubbles, of laser-guided rockets and bombs, striking extremely small, precisely targeted, sites.

OPPENHEIMER *enters, uncertainly. He wears cowboy boots, wide-brimmed hat, blue jeans. Enters, stops, looks, goes to card table, stops, looks, sits, shuffles.*]

OPPENHEIMER VOICE-OVER: Dear Professor Bridgman, you may remember that when I was at Harvard two years ago I was very much interested in your theory of metallic conduction. Recently in the course of some work in quantum mechanics that I have been pursuing at Göttingen, an idea has turned up which seems to offer a certain support to your theory. I think it will be some time before a complete quantum theory of conduction is possible, but perhaps I may tell you briefly of this one point.

[*While he shuffles and his voice-over is heard,* VON NEUMANN, TELLER, *and* FERMI *enter, some moments apart, and take their places around the table: All wear sunglasses. Teller wears heavy gloves, welder's goggles. Fermi wears white laboratory overalls. Von Neumann dresses like a banker, in three-piece suit, pocket handkerchief. Eventually, Oppenheimer deals. While all this goes on, the voice-over continues.*]

A DIFFERENT VOICE-OVER: I hope you will pardon my presumption, but I have taken the liberty of drawing up a revised Ten Commandments, since the old ten haven't worked so well.

First. Recognize the connections of things and the laws of the conduct of men, so that you may know what you are doing. This is an important one. Try not to forget it. You may begin, for instance, with a thought of what you are doing and find, soon enough, that someone else has taken over the direction of your work and what you thought was fine and pure, extraordinary even, has become mundane or dreadful. Or not even that someone else has taken it over, but that some other aspect in your own character has. As, for instance, fear. Or vanity. Lust for power. Et cetera.

Second. Let your acts be directed toward a worthy goal, but do not ask if they will reach it. They are to be models and examples, that's all. This is an important one, too—though harder to get at first. I could elaborate, but I think I ought simply to leave this one to you to consider.

Third. Speak to all men as you do to yourself, with no concern for the effect you make, so that you don't shut them out from your world; lest in isolation the meaning of life slips out of sight and you lose the belief in the perfection of creation. You see what I mean.

Fourth. Do not destroy what you cannot create. Do not destroy what you cannot create.

Fifth. Lead your life with a gentle hand and be ready to leave whenever you are called. That one is for the poets. Others are welcome to it, of course, as they wish.

Sixth. Do your work for six years; but in the seventh, go into solitude or among strangers, so that the recollection of your friends does not hide you from seeing what you have become. This is a personal one. Crucial, I think.

Seventh. Do not covet what you cannot have. Also personal. And not personal at the same time.

Eighth. This is an important one again: do not add to the madness. If you can't stop it, at least do not help to push it over the edge. That's obvious enough, hardly worth stating. I wouldn't state it if we weren't all so forgetful.

[*They bet before they look at their hands.*]

OPPENHEIMER: Bets?

VON NEUMANN: Five dollars.

TELLER: Five and raise you fifty.

FERMI: Are you going to cheat?

TELLER: Why do you say that?

FERMI: I know something about odds.

TELLER: I have a fantastic hand.

FERMI: Evidently.

OPPENHEIMER: Bets?

FERMI: Do you think I'd bet in a game like this?

OPPENHEIMER: I only ask.

FERMI: One hundred dollars.

VON NEUMANN: I don't know.

FERMI: Well, you have to estimate. What's the fun in life if you don't estimate. For instance. Take a problem. Let us say: how many barbers are there in the United States? How many piano tuners are there in Chicago? What is the number of sheep in Nevada? These things can be quantified. Try and make an estimate within a factor of ten. Take another problem. How many locomotives are there in America?

TELLER: This is quite boring.

FERMI: Within an order of magnitude. First, how many miles do you have to drive before crossing a railroad track, on the average? From this number you obtain the number of miles of railroad track in America.

TELLER: I don't need to listen to this.

FERMI: Third, estimate the number of miles of track per locomotive. And there you have it.

TELLER: Who cares about this?

FERMI: You remember Archimedes' famous experiment where he measured the amount of gold in a crown by putting it in a tub of water to see how much water it displaced. One may measure anything in this way: a crown, an automobile, a human being. The water doesn't know the difference. I did the same thing with my Nobel Prize, for instance, and I must say I was pleased to find that it had a gold content. These Nobel Prizes are not entirely worthless after all. I was able, in fact, to do the same thing with my wedding presents. The first step is to identify what it is to be measured. That's the essential point. If you go wrong there, you've gone wrong, and that's all there is to it. You may say that the beauty of life is its complexity. And I would say, yes! And also the beauty of life is its simplicity.

TELLER: Locomotives. Crowns. Wedding presents. Does one care about these things any more?

VON NEUMANN: It makes one giddy to think about these things, I think. If anyone says he can think about quantum theory without getting giddy, he hasn't understood the first thing about it. One mustn't discount the miraculous aspect. One doesn't want to reduce the mysteries to a mere game.

OPPENHEIMER: Dealer is in.

FERMI: What do you think are my chances of becoming Pope? For instance, how would you calculate that?

TELLER: I think it would be a miracle.

FERMI: Precisely. And what is a miracle? Offhand, I would define a miracle as an event which has a probability of less than ten percent. Rabi said to me: look, these things ought to be kept secret. Because you know what it might lead to.

[*He laughs.*]

Nuts! I said to him. Nuts! Well, he said, what do you estimate are the proba-bilities? Remote, I said. Remote, he said, what do you mean by this word re-mote? Well, I said: remote, that would be ten per cent. Ten percent, he said. That is not remote, I think, if it has consequences!

[*He laughs.*]

Fortunately, for me no emotion lasts more than two minutes.

OPPENHEIMER: Lord, these affairs are hard on the heart.

FERMI: Of course this ten percent factor is reversible, too. I wouldn't say it's not.

OPPENHEIMER: Cards?

FERMI: Three cards.

VON NEUMANN: Two cards.

[*Through the remainder of the scene we hear the sounds of radar, a NASA launch preparation, remarks of casino dealers, crap tables, pilots talking to each other, control tower talk.*]

TELLER: Of course, you may speculate all you want about these things, but it all comes down finally to a world where animals eat one another, doesn't it? If you choose to think of it in a certain way: we are waging a war against all the nonhuman animals, aren't we?

FERMI: That's a bit extreme, isn't it?

TELLER: Do you think so?

FERMI: Well, we aren't food faddists, are we?

VON NEUMANN: I should hope not.

FERMI: Well, there you have it.

TELLER: Indeed. One cares about what works, there's my point. Physics is interested in an estimation of forces.

OPPENHEIMER: When one says that now we physicists have known sin, I don't think we have, in some particular sense, committed an act that is wrong or bad. Rather, I think what is meant is that we have entered a realm that was always forbidden to us as human beings, a realm that was reserved to the gods, or, if you prefer, to the universe itself, and that our entrance into that forbidden realm was sacrilege. Now we see the punishment for it. We've transformed our home into the most perilous place in the universe. Not even a dog would do that. So that now, our fondest dream as a species is to leave the earth. We think of nothing else.

TELLER: Nonsense. I think of other things all the time. I think of what works.

OPPENHEIMER: We've had the lifespan of butterflies really.

VON NEUMANN: Cards?

TELLER: No cards.

OPPENHEIMER: Dealer takes one. Bets?

TELLER: One thousand dollars.

FERMI: Of course, if you're going to cheat, there would be no point in going on.

TELLER: That would be up to you.

FERMI: I find anything other than an honest game uninteresting.

TELLER: Each to his own taste, to be sure.

FERMI: Tennis without a net is pointless, surely.

TELLER: In what sense?

FERMI: Where is the mathematics then? What is the point?

TELLER: What is the point of mathematics?

FERMI: It is its own end.

TELLER: That is a matter of taste, surely. The point, really, is beating you.

FERMI: I have a parlor game I sometimes play with friends called Murder. The rules are very simple. First, you turn out the lights. Second is poking. Third is kissing. Fourth lights on again. And then you determine who is the murderer.

TELLER: How do you do that?

FERMI: Well, we already know: you are.

TELLER: This is an ugly thing to say.

FERMI: We all know you have no sense of fun, no sense of play.

TELLER: Is this meant to be a charge against me? Will you condemn a grown man because he doesn't like finger painting?

FERMI: Must a man be so homicidally serious to be a man?

TELLER: I'm a logical person. I'm simply a logical person. What sort of madman would consider this a charge?

VON NEUMANN: Consider your logic. Is it sufficiently inclusive. For example, it is clear that neither a pencil-stroke nor a steamship is simple. Is there really a logical equivalence between these two?

OPPENHEIMER: Are there bets?

VON NEUMANN: I fold.

FERMI: What is the point? I'm out.

OPPENHEIMER: I'll see you and raise you a thousand.

TELLER: See and raise a thousand.

FERMI: What are the probabilities of both having winning hands?

VON NEUMANN: Where $y1s$-$y1s(p)$ is the expected payoff for player one of his strategy p against player two's actual hand s and actual choice ig equals i, then $K(p/o)$ equals $1/Sy1y1s$.

OPPENHEIMER: Are you still in this game?

VON NEUMANN: In a certain narrow sense. Shall I explain the rules to you?

OPPENHEIMER: Please. Be so kind.

VON NEUMANN: In game theory it is assumed that both players have examined all the strategies before the game begins and have also decided which strategy to take. The play itself is consequently completely mechanical and predetermined. The value of the game lies in attaining both the smallest maximum and the largest minimum—one and negative one. This theory applies only to games where the players have full information of the state of the game at any time during the game—tic-tac-toe, checkers, and chess. For games such as paper, scissors, stone, or poker, one must add the word average to the value of the game. I can recommend for games of incomplete information only a sound policy for many rounds. The best strategy, then, is random and mixed such that the largest minimum of average payoff to A obtains and coincides with the smallest maximum of the average payoff to B, and this value is the unique average value of the game. There is no best strategy for one round. One can play or not play, but the game goes on in any case, with new players replacing the old; and it has its own logic on which the players are carried along with ever-increasing stakes. There are no exact parallels since the play is ever-intensifying. The players cannot affect the game, although the game can affect the players.

TELLER: Will you deal?

[OPPENHEIMER *again shuffles.*]

[*The light is such that the silver screen glistens like a metal of the distant future. Green fog pervades the stage.*
    THE PHYSICISTS *all descend through trap doors. The* DEAD SOLDIER *rises through a trap door, holding an empty red pottery vase, stands silently.*

Space music. Very strange, violent, and beautiful. Projections of stars, bubble chambers—very beautiful. Projections of microscopic underwater life forms of all kinds—very beautiful. Sounds and images that call up an unreasoning love of the earth, other space sounds—but these very beautiful. Finger cymbals. Whale songs.]

THE END

The Investigation of the Murder in El Salvador

The Investigation of the Murder in El Salvador was developed with director Peter Brosius in a workshop production at the Mark Taper Forum in Los Angeles and had its first full production, under a grant from the Fund for New American Plays, at New York Theatre Workshop, where it was directed by David Schweizer.

The Investigation of the
Murder in El Salvador

While the audience waits for the piece to begin: the sound of ocean waves, the occasional call of a tropical bird.

Music, interspersed and overlaid with other sounds, plays throughout the piece. It should begin the piece, as an overture of five or ten minutes, to set an estranged opening viewpoint.

The lights come up slowly on a vast, white space, with overtones of tropical pink, orange, crimson. To one side is an astonishingly large vase of fresh flowers. A sense of perfect cleanness, simplicity, and purity.

Seven people are on stage, all with their heads slightly turned, listening intently. Two men, GALLEJAS *and* STANTON, *sit on cushioned white wicker chairs. The men wear white linen suits.* GALLEJAS *wears white gloves and yellow (sunlight) tinted glasses.* STANTON *wears glasses tinted pink.*

They will speak first—and as they talk, projections of them, seated in various postures, as though they are pictures from a fashion magazine, are shown on a screen that fills the entire rear stage. The projections fall on various places on the screen. Some are simultaneous, spill over one another; others are projected from the side and distorted.

From time to time during the course of the piece, sentences will appear in moving lights; these are meant to look like the lights for the news of the world above Times Square.

Many of the silences indicated throughout the script, whether long or short, should feel as though a life has ended, the actors drift away into their preoccupations, and then society is reconstituted, with the actors having drifted to new thoughts.

GALLEJAS *is half English and half Spanish or West Indian.* STANTON *is American Presbyterian.*

In another similar wicker chair slightly removed from them sits LADY AITKEN *with her Lhasa Apso in her lap. She, too, is dressed in white, with a straw hat.*

Her husband HOWARD *sits all the way upstage at dead center, apart from all the rest, alone, in a wheelchair. He has had a stroke and holds his drink in one hand that is suspended from a sling that keeps it near his lips. He wears beige. He will not speak at all for the first forty minutes. (If it is thought that the audience requires more biographical information about Howard, his biographical sketch can be passed out with the program.) Just next to Howard stands a bodyguard in dark suit, arms folded, dark sunglasses. On a chaise longue is* MERIDEE, *a young woman, stretched out getting a sun tan. She wears pastels. Seated on the end of the chaise is* PETER, *a young man in white and pastels. At the opening* PETER *is applying sun tan lotion to Meridee. Later he will apply a white facial made of lime blossom extract, which she will keep to the end.*

These characters are all drinking a red drink. They eat throughout, choosing from copious amounts of fresh fruits, cheeses, delicacies.

As we shall see, the cast also includes a black butler and two maids.

STANTON [*To Gallejas*]: Did you hear that?

GALLEJAS: What?

STANTON: That scream.

GALLEJAS: Ah. Yes.

STANTON: I couldn't tell whether it came from inside or out.

GALLEJAS: No.

[*They are silent, listening.*]

STANTON: I was saying. About the Englishman who was instructing me to hold my bat. We were on a green in a small village near London, in the direction of Oxford. A sunny day. He was dressed in flannels, quite correct. In point of fact, I was extremely happy, so that I was surprised when the Englishman, in showing me how to handle one sort of pitch or another, suddenly said, "If you miss them all, then just throw your bat at the pitcher's head"— and with that, he threw his bat with terrific force directly at my head, barely missed me, and shouted, "Run!" "But," I said, "That's not cricket." "Cricket!" he said, "I'm talking about how to get to first base."

[GALLEJAS *laughs happily and too long. The call of a tropical bird is heard. Pictures of Lady Aitken join the projections.*]

LADY AITKEN: I went to Saks the other day, and I saw—I don't think I've ever seen them anywhere before—very large, eighteenth-century Chinese wall hangings, all in silk, brilliant reds and blues and yellows, vast silks, four-by-eight feet, beautifully woven, with beautiful moire patterns, scintillating, appearing and disappearing as the silks billowed out from the wall, and the silks had on them the faces and figures of famous Chinese actors and actresses.

STANTON: Amazing.

LADY AITKEN: And no one was buying them! I couldn't understand it. And then I realized: no one knew what to do with them. No one could even imagine how to get them home. They were so big. No one knew how to fold them. Only I knew the secret: a very rare technique for wrapping them around a bamboo pole to take them home with me. And I took one. I took the red silk, and wrapped myself up inside it, and now you can see what's happened to me!

GALLEJAS: What?

LADY AITKEN: I came out a butterfly!

[*All laugh, too long.*]

STANTON: Ah!
[*A silence*]
Yes.
[*He smiles.*]
Aren't we all butterflies, really?

[*All laugh again. As the conversation continues, pictures are projected of twelve stages in the preparation of a Mediterranean sea bass.*]

STANTON: Have you ever been to Howrah?

GALLEJAS [*After a moment*]: Across the Hooghly River from Calcutta.

STANTON: Yes.

GALLEJAS [*After a moment*]: Trading center.

STANTON: Since 1560.

GALLEJAS: Dusty roads.

STANTON: Old warehouses . . .

GALLEJAS: Called godowns.

STANTON: That's the place, yes.

GALLEJAS: Street dwellers huddling under thin blankets at night.

STANTON: Yes. On cool evenings, sometimes, rats will crawl under the blankets, apparently to get warm.

GALLEJAS: Evidently. We had a factory there.

STANTON: Yes. So do we. Some of the workers sleep in the godowns.

GALLEJAS: I did myself.

STANTON: Really?

GALLEJAS: Dark, dusty place, hot, made rather unpleasant by the cockroaches, thousands of large brown ones, flew about in the dark and kept getting into my hair.

STANTON: Nasty business.

GALLEJAS: Yes. At times, more than a hundred rats would be feeding in my room at one time.

STANTON: Bandicoot rats, were they?

GALLEJAS: Lesser bandicoot rats, *Bandicota bengalensis*. The adults are seven-and-a-half inches long, excluding the tail. Blunted snouts. Rarely more than ten ounces in weight. Otherwise they resemble the Norway rat. You've seen them, I'm sure.

STANTON: Of course.

GALLEJAS: Found from Nepal to Sri Lanka, from Pakistan to Indonesia.

STANTON: Extraordinary.

GALLEJAS: Dominant in Calcutta, Bombay, Madras.

STANTON: I should have thought so.

GALLEJAS: Feed on wheat, rice, garbage, insects, dead birds. Preferred wheat or rice actually. Drank from the gutter, or sometimes from the nearby latrines. At times I could watch them there drinking my urine.

STANTON: Really?

GALLEJAS: They didn't go out of their way to bother me, I must say. They investigated me, of course, as they would any object, walking over me, sniffing. Licking. That's all. Sometimes one of the boys I was with would kick one of them, or even beat it to death.

STANTON: Really? Why was that?

GALLEJAS: No point to it, really.

[*Gallejas laughs. All laugh. A black* BUTLER *enters, passes a tray heaped with little sandwiches.* GALLEJAS *waves them away.* STANTON *carefully chooses a single one. The laughter of a myna bird.*]

GALLEJAS [*To butler*]: You didn't scream a moment ago?

BUTLER: No, sir.

GALLEJAS: Do you know who did?

BUTLER: I don't know, sir. It must have been one of the maids.

GALLEJAS: Will you ask her to see me when she has a moment.

BUTLER: Yes, sir.
[*Long silence*]
Will that be all, sir?

GALLEJAS: Yes, thank you.

[*They are silent until the* BUTLER *leaves.*]

STANTON: Of course they're not easy to prepare.

GALLEJAS: Not easy to bone.

STANTON: Not that hard to bone, but how would you have them? Filets sauteed with butter, perhaps?

GALLEJAS: A light cream sauce.

LADY AITKEN: I think you might do them as one does quail.

STANTON: How is that?

LADY AITKEN: Well, I don't cook, dear, but however one does quail is how one would do rat. I think.

MERIDEE: I'm ready for dessert!

STANTON: Haven't we eaten dessert?

GALLEJAS [*Politely*]: What will you have?

MERIDEE [*Bored*]: Well, I know what I want: a sort of an ice cream soda, in a tall, fluted, crystal goblet, very large, very tall, and very big around, you know what I mean?

GALLEJAS: Yes.

MERIDEE: And it is brought to me.

GALLEJAS: Yes.

MERIDEE: And then, after it is set down on the table in front of me, then the ice cream is put into it—four, five, six scoops, maybe eight scoops, vanilla, and chocolate, fudge swirl, strawberry, something with nuts . . .

[*In moving lights:* What was she doing here? Had she been so bored where she had been? And thought this might be interesting?]

GALLEJAS: Black walnuts . . .

MERIDEE: Right, or maple fudge nut.

GALLEJAS: Yes.

LADY AITKEN: I don't know.

MERIDEE: And when the ice cream is put in, then the whole thing reacts like an atomic bomb—I mean the tumult and the churning and the shaft rising up . . .

GALLEJAS: Yes?

MERIDEE: And the swirling turmoil, the mushroom cap on top—oh, it's amazing, you've never seen anything like it; you can see through the sides of the glass the beautiful swirling and churning, powerful, intricate, complex movements, and it goes on and on and on, after you think it can't go on any longer, it still does, going on and on. I'm a visceral person.

[*Sound of a helicopter overhead. A long silence. To Stanton.*]

What are you having for dessert?

STANTON: Oh . . . I . . . hadn't thought about it.

MERIDEE: Think about it.

STANTON: Well . . . I think I might have a chocolate mousse.

MERIDEE: Unh-hunh.

STANTON: [*Voice through loudspeaker or directly to audience*]: I saw at once that she was disappointed by my choice, so I tried to improve it.

STANTON: I see it arriving, being brought in from the kitchen on the back of a horse, and I get up to go and meet the horse and take its lead rope to bring it to the table.

MERIDEE: It's the only way to serve a mousse, really, if you don't want it to bore you to death.

PETER: The other night at Nigel's, they served Jamaican food, while a Jamaican band played steel drums and penny whistles. You know, yams, sweet potatoes, lentils, all warm and steamy, and it all smelled wonderful, such a wonderful warm, happy, satisfying meal, and when they brought in the main course, I knew it would be exquisite, and I had to smell it right away, it smelled so good, and somehow quite familiar. "Why!" I said, "It smells like shit!" "Yes, sir," said the maid. And it was! Jamaican shit!

[*He gives a long, loud shrill, whinnying laugh, hoping he has impressed Meridee. No one else laughs. He subsides.*]

MERIDEE [*To audience*]: I don't think of myself as rich. I think of myself as comfortable, yes, but not rich.

PETER: Well no, yes. I mean no. Doesn't everybody?

THE ACTORS *sit, silent, all looking out at audience. Music: Beautiful, quiet, pure—Brian Eno perhaps. Voice-over: A quiet, soft, female voice, a monologue: instructions on how to care for a gun.*

Projections: A movie of a young woman at a health spa, with stills, on a second scrim, of the same young woman.

NOTES ON INTERLUDES IN GENERAL: These interludes "bleed" both ways—that is to say, they may begin before the preceding scene is completed, and the succeeding scene may begin before the interlude has been concluded. Usually, just one element of the interlude will bleed to form a bridge between the preceding and succeeding scenes.

During the ensuing scene, Meridee, restless, tries lying first one way and then another, gets up, paces, lies down on terrace in front of others, turns over, drapes herself over the chaise, etc.

LADY AITKEN: Do you swim?

GALLEJAS: Of course. In hot water.

LADY AITKEN: It's the only sport I can do, really. Good for my back.

GALLEJAS: Yes.

STANTON: I swim when I'm in Greece, Corsica, the Porto Rotondo. Off Cavallo.

LADY AITKEN: Do you swim the breast stroke?

STANTON: Yes.

LADY AITKEN: It's my favorite stroke. I like to do the breast stroke in the nude, don't you?

STANTON: No.

[*In moving lights:* And why had she come with him? Could it have been a casual affair?]

LADY AITKEN: I like to swim at night. Howard and I used to swim in the bay at Acapulco. That used to be my favorite for swimming at night. Not now, of course. Sometimes I go into a pool now, the one at the Hotel Nikko. But I much prefer to swim off the yacht near the Turkish Islands. With my little surfboard. I hold it and kick my legs behind. Don't you love the feeling of being able to swim and swim anywhere?

STANTON: I usually stay in one area, actually.
[*One beat.*]
Fear of sharks.

[*Silence.*]

LADY AITKEN: To me, swimming is like being baptized. It just washes away all your sins and troubles.

[HOWARD *looks up, around, back down.*]

LADY AITKEN [*Politely*]: Do you shoot?

GALLEJAS: Of course.

LADY AITKEN: La Chasse is out.

GALLEJAS: Certainly not.

LADY AITKEN: I think you'll find it is.

[*As Lady Aitken continues to speak, super-realist still life paintings by Jeanette Pasin Sloan are projected: Diet-Rite, 7-Up, Heller mug.*]

Loose face powder is in.
Linen bath towels are in.
But la chasse is out.

STANTON: Ah-ha.

LADY AITKEN: Swiss bank accounts are out, as you know, I'm sure.
Loulou de Waldner is in again.
Omelettes are out. Too bad.
But mashed potatoes are in.

STANTON: Ah-ha.

MERIDEE: The Forties are out.

LADY AITKEN: Surfing is out.

MERIDEE: Belgium is out.

LADY AITKEN: Scotland is in.

MERIDEE: Fucking is out, although you wouldn't know it, the way people talk about it all the time.

LADY AITKEN: Chintz is out.

MERIDEE: Owning your own island is in, for sure, and I can see why, too.

STANTON: Small dinner parties at a round table are in, I think.

LADY AITKEN: Blue hydrangeas are in.

GALLEJAS: Collecting old airplanes is in.

STANTON: Dining in your greenhouse is in.

PETER: Sicily is in.

LADY AITKEN [*Gently*]: No, dear, Sicily is out.

GALLEJAS: Hunt breakfasts are in.

STANTON: And whale-watching.

LADY AITKEN: Tiny cookies at tea time are in,
White cotton Indian nightdresses are in.
And letter writing.
And fringe.
But loofah sponges are out.

GALLEJAS: That's too bad.

LADY AITKEN: Chopin nocturnes are in. The Bristol Hotel in Paris.
Placing your furniture at an angle is out.
The rock-hard derriere is out.

MERIDEE: No, the rock-hard derriere is still in, you can take my word for it.

LADY AITKEN: Oh?

MERIDEE: And firm thighs.
And the exposed back is in,
you can count on it.

LADY AITKEN: Really?

MERIDEE: Walking your mother is in, too, I'm told.

LADY AITKEN: Uh-huh.
[*Resuming.*]
Floral sachets in the closet are in.

MERIDEE: Bachelors are out. Face it. You know what I mean.

LADY AITKEN: Long nails are out, too, really.

PETER: Onion soup is out.

LADY AITKEN: Yes.
Bonsai cherry trees are in.

STANTON: Swedish antiques are in, I think.

MERIDEE: Caviar is out.

LADY AITKEN: Thoughtfulness is in.
Lunch under an apple tree is in.
Politics are out.

[*The music eases into the sound of ocean waves.*]

LADY AITKEN: I've seen all the inaugural parades, you know, since McKinley.
We watched the McKinley parade from our rooms in the Blackstone—or is
that Chicago? After a while, they all look alike. The motorcars change, the
dresses change, but nothing else changes. After a while, you think: well, what
difference does it make? And: what can I do about it? After the First War, the
peasants cut down my family's woods in Vienna to use for firewood. It was
dreadful.

STANTON: That they cut down the trees.

LADY AITKEN: Yes.

[*In moving lights:* But was this fun? Were these her kind of people, after all?]

MERIDEE: That they suffered so.

GALLEJAS: The peasants.

LADY AITKEN: Yes! It was such a crime.

STANTON: What woods were they?

LADY AITKEN: The Vienna woods.

STANTON: The Vienna woods belonged to your family?

LADY AITKEN: Well, we're all immigrants, aren't we?

[*The sound of ocean waves. Several moments silence.*]

MERIDEE: Let's talk about your servants.

GALLEJAS: Ah, yes. They're from Rhodesia. Trained by the English.

MERIDEE: You don't like the locals?

GALLEJAS: They're rather too tied-in with the situation.

STANTON: What do they want, anyway? What do servants want?

GALLEJAS: I don't think you can blame the servants.

LADY AITKEN: I don't think you can blame Howard.

GALLEJAS [*Sharply*]: I haven't blamed Howard.

STANTON: I don't think I'm at fault.

PETER: Sometimes the way they look at you, you think you might be at fault.

STANTON: At me?
[*Beat*]
Well. How do they manage? I sometimes wonder.

PETER: Of course, servants are a different thing from peasants. For a lot of these people, this is the choice they've made, after all.

[*Silence*]

STANTON [*Uncertainly*]: Yes. Indeed.

LADY AITKEN: Annie Whitlaw was raped, you know.

GALLEJAS: After her massage.

LADY AITKEN: In Rhodesia.

GALLEJAS: Not the place to fall asleep.

LADY AITKEN: I don't think you can say it was Annie Whitlaw's fault.

PETER: Do you sleep with a gun?

LADY AITKEN: I think it's in their genes.

MERIDEE: Genes? I think it's in their toilet training. They have this very macho toilet training where the mothers smear feces on the babies' faces.

PETER: Who is this?

MERIDEE: The natives.

PETER: Is this true?

STANTON: Surely it's more organizational. Historical, perhaps, really.

LADY AITKEN: Well, of course. Isn't everything?

MERIDEE: You mean the way the English have treated them?

LADY AITKEN [*Very carefully*]: Treated? I wouldn't say that. The English are a very decent people really.

STANTON: Indeed.

LADY AITKEN: They suffer for it.

STANTON [*Almost catching her drift*]: The English.

LADY AITKEN: Who?

STANTON: Suffer for it.

LADY AITKEN: Yes. I sometimes think that's why they indulge themselves so in food and drink and comfort.

[*Silence. No one comprehends.*]

They need an anesthetic.

[*Insisting*] It's not a good situation. The natives are enraged, and the English are anesthetized. And these are graduates of Oxford and Cambridge, mind you. These are people who have read philosophy and history and poetry. They have studied astronomy. They have read the Bhagavad Gita. These are the finest minds that have chosen to spend their lives half asleep. This is a tragic situation. It is as though you were to take a fine piece of crystal and just throw it to the floor and shatter it.

[*Silence. The call of a tropical bird. The actors ruminate. The call of a myna bird.*]

GALLEJAS: Yes, well, history makes neurosis. We repress things. Nothing personal in it.

STANTON: No. One can't be too careful.

GALLEJAS: It's not a pleasant continent, Africa.

MERIDEE: This isn't such a pleasant continent either!

[*The* BUTLER *enters. A movie is projected during the following scene and then on through the succeeding interlude: of a black man running away in the countryside.*]

BUTLER: I beg your pardon, sir, but I wonder if I could speak with you for a moment.

GALLEJAS: It is a bit awkward just now. Can it wait?

BUTLER: Oh, yes, sir, I think it can, sir. Certainly, sir, if you wish.

[*Silence. All look at the butler and wonder, Is he too obsequious?*]

Projections of a black man assaulting his wife. A half dozen still shots of a man beating a woman. Done fairly quickly, in a count of six or eight.]

[*In moving lights:* And had she meant to stay with Peter this long, really?]

GALLEJAS: Weren't you going to send in one of the maids?

BUTLER: Yes, sir, if you wish, I certainly shall.

GALLEJAS: That is what I wish, yes.

BUTLER: Right away, sir?

GALLEJAS: Right away.

BUTLER [*After a pause*]: Will that be all, sir?

[*Long silence*]

GALLEJAS: Yes.

BUTLER: Thank you, sir.

[*He leaves. All are silent. Terrified.*]

[THE ACTORS *watch* GALLEJAS, *who, having finished eating a piece of fruit, washes his hands very slowly and carefully in a silver bowl of water and dries his hands equally slowly and thoroughly. Music: Quiet. Contemplative. With the sound of distant jet planes high above.*]

VOICE-OVER [*A soft, female voice, calm, beautiful, and matter of fact*]: With Saturn now passing over the mid-heaven point of your solar chart no one can say you are not totally dedicated and personally ambitious. In fact, they may well complain you have been something of a workaholic of late. Only you realize how important it is for you to consolidate your position. But you really do need to find time to relax and unwind this month, especially during the first three weeks while the Sun remains in the grueling sign of Capricorn. Astrological tradition has it that this is when your physical resources are at their lowest and you are prone to minor ailments. Also, when Mercury, the planet of the mind, turns to retrograde motion in your own sign on the 8th, you could fail to notice storm warnings in close personal relationships and end up having to say you are sorry—something Aquarians find almost impossible to do.

[*Projections: Models in handcuffs, swimsuits in bombed-out buildings, models holding rifles, modeling camouflage fashions. These projections bleed into the following scene.*]

[*Projected quotation:* We go to the stud sales. We don't just sit around. I can tell you that.]

[*The sound of a jet tears across the sky from one side to the other.*]

PETER [*Laughing uneasily*]: Of course we don't have a servant problem in New York. I mean, I have a cleaning woman, of course, but she doesn't live in. Your servants live in.

GALLEJAS: Yes.

PETER: You must trust them.

[*Long silence*]

GALLEJAS: No.

MERIDEE: How many servants do you have?

GALLEJAS: Five.

MERIDEE: Do they rape you quite a lot?

GALLEJAS: Not me, often. Young white women are another thing, of course.

MERIDEE: How do they do it, I wonder.

GALLEJAS: With their cocks, I'm told.

LADY AITKEN: Charles!

GALLEJAS: I don't think there's much fist fucking in this part of the world.

LADY AITKEN [*Rising*]: Really!

GALLEJAS: Buggery is another matter. I think 73 percent of all sex acts involve buggery these days.

LADY AITKEN: Charles!

PETER [*Concerned*]: Do they really?

MERIDEE: Are you afraid?

GALLEJAS: Not for myself, although, since I've come to know you, I often think of you in this context.

MERIDEE: What a delightful luncheon this is turning out to be.

[*Projection:* I should really live in Cuba, I love sugar so.]

MERIDEE: What do you do all day?

GALLEJAS: Do?

MERIDEE: Yes. All day.

GALLEJAS: I give advice, mostly. Nothing official. Technical questions, you know: what to do with the bodies, that sort of thing.

[MERIDEE *laughs.*]

What do you do?

MERIDEE: I sunbathe.

GALLEJAS: Ah-ha.

MERIDEE: You know, I've gotten to the point where I change my clothes thirteen times a day. I'm getting to feel like a real professional. But I am learning how to control my quim muscles.

STANTON: Your what?

MERIDEE: My quim muscles. You know. I can make the muscles in my quim contract and move back and forth until it comes inside-out. My quim comes right out, like a man.

STANTON: Ah-ha.
[*Beat*]
Well. Extraordinary.

PETER [*Still caught up in a sort of delayed action, in the excitement*]: Last night at a dinner party I got into the most incredible conversation where this guy across the table was telling me that he had tied up a whore in Mexico one time and carved the chart of the year's Dow Jones averages into her, starting at her navel and going right around her torso and back to her navel—up and down, a whole year's worth. Is that incredible?

[*Silence*]

MERIDEE: Yes.

[*Silence*]

PETER: Look, don't try to make me out some kind of Goebbels or something. I happen to be a very average sort of person, with very average, typical sort of stuff, very sort of usual human feelings. I mean, if you can't see the humor in what that guy did then you're just cut off from half the people in the world. I mean, some things are funny even if they're not nice. I mean, this is the real world. Look, I'm as nice as people get.

[*Silence*]

MERIDEE: I should be working in a general store in Vermont.

PETER: Well, you're hard to figure sometimes, but we've had some wonderful times together.

MERIDEE: Who?

PETER: You and I.

MERIDEE: Are you kidding? Are you entirely conscious?

PETER: You're goddamn right. Mexico. Lake Tahoe. Aspen that time.
[*Beat*]
The Orange Bowl.
[*Beat*]
I mean, I'm not a dumb person. I'm not an insensitive person. I'm a human being, too. Some people think I'm very smart. I remember numbers, for instance. I have a head for figures. I remember when three month–money was at 19 percent at the same time it was 6 in Japan, 9 in West Germany, 7 and 3/5 in Holland, 12 and 3/5 in France, 15 in Belgium, 11 in Britain, 11 in the U.S., 8 in Switzerland. I remember that. At the same time that government bonds were 4.22 in Switzerland, 19.18 in Italy. I play tennis. I've read Rosenstock-Huessy. I'm not at a loss for dinner companions. Some people think I'm quite funny.

PETER: [*Voice on loudspeaker or directly as narrator*]: Just then I noticed something was gripping my left leg. I put my hand down to see what the trouble was, and I felt something furry. I looked down. A small dog was biting my leg. That was a surprise. I tried to jerk my leg away from the dog, but the dog, a little Lhasa Apso, a scrappy little dog, had a good bite on my leg and wouldn't let go. I can't say that it hurt very much; it hurt a little, sure; but mostly it was tremendously irritating. The dog was on a leash. He belonged to Lady Aitken.

PETER: Pardon me,

PETER'S VOICE: I said to her.

PETER: Is that your dog?

LADY AITKEN: Yes,

PETER'S VOICE: she said, turning back to her champagne.

PETER: Well, look,

PETER'S VOICE: I said,

PETER: your dog is biting me.

PETER'S VOICE: She got upset at that. I guess I had somehow rubbed her the wrong way.

PETER: Your dog is biting my leg.

LADY AITKEN [*Looks at Peter, looks at the dog, back to Peter.*]: He is not.

PETER [*Screaming*]: Your dog is biting my leg!

LADY AITKEN: You're screaming.

PETER: He's biting my leg!

[*She looks at him evenly. He speaks quietly.*]

Call off your dog!

LADY AITKEN: My dog is not doing you any harm.

PETER [*Quietly*]: Anybody in the world could see that your dog is biting my fucking leg.

LADY AITKEN: This conversation has gone far enough.

PETER [*Calmly*]: Let's start this one from the beginning. I'm going to kill your dog. I'm going to bash his head in with a hammer.

LADY AITKEN: You don't have a hammer.

PETER'S VOICE: But, I did have a hammer. I took it from my pocket, and I said,

PETER: But I do have a hammer, right here, and I am going to bash his head in.

LADY AITKEN: Here, boy,

PETER'S VOICE: she said—
and the dog let go.

HOWARD [*A long laugh*]: I've always worked with decent people, whatever the situation I've been in, however bad things have gotten: you think people were always animals but that's bullshit bullshit because I have never been associated with anyone but people who have read Plato St. Augustine that sort of thing Acquinas even I'm talking about you know what's-his-name Penny knows I'm talking about Averell, I don't care what you might think well, sure, a man with that kind of money, you know, 300, 400 shirts in every closet but that's bullshit bullshit because even Averell comparatively speaking. And he returned my phone calls.

Hello Governor, I would say, Hello Howard he would say because he knew me he knew me starting back with Stevenson and then you know Birmingham, the marches Lyndon Johnson the whole fucking thing I could tell you stories. One has vanity after all, this is no sin, one likes to be with powerful people. Even Albert Schweitzer liked to be with powerful people. Oppenheimer you know: a very civilized man. A very civilized man. We talked about the moon program, and he got up and stepped to this blackboard he had in his office and wrote out an equation on the blackboard and he said: Now we know this to be true, don't you think it's vulgar to spend all this money simply to demonstrate it? You know one likes to be with civilized people. But you people haven't been anywhere. You people haven't seen these places. I'm talking about Clare Booth Luce's house with Bush and Buckley and Al Haig I mean some of these people I've lived with were animals I'm talking about Colby and Teller, fucking Kraut, you know a real Kraut. Fourteen rooms, and lanais and atriums and baths, God it was hard to secure, that house.

CLARE BOOTH LUCE'S VOICE [*Over loudspeaker*]: Military people love me,

HOWARD: she said,

LUCE'S VOICE: and I love them.

HOWARD: She even said she might marry again.

LUCE'S VOICE: But only if I find a handsome, retired, homosexual admiral.

[*Movie continues as Howard continues to talk.*]

HOWARD: But you haven't seen the backs of the heads blown off, brains leaking through your fingers like Jello, flies, flies all in the mouth, in the ears, flies in the nostrils, the eye sockets inside the skull—they fly up against your lips, cheeks—and dogs tearing away the flesh, you've never seen such dogs where you come from, pulling flesh from bone, until your head is so filled with these pictures that it has to explode!!

[*Silence*]

And then, when they'd finished with me, they threw me away like an old dog. Well, I always planned to get out anyway, as soon as I could.

[*Silence*]

STANTON: Well, I'm getting out as soon as I can.

LADY AITKEN [*Studying Stanton closely*]: Have you had plastic surgery?

STANTON: Certainly not.

LADY AITKEN: Just a little tuck in the fat pockets around the lower lids.

[*In moving lights:* Was her sense of revulsion entirely aesthetic?]

STANTON: Certainly not.

LADY AITKEN: Are you afraid of the complications?

GALLEJAS [*Absently*]: Blood clots. Scarring.

[*Projection:* Her Majesty and I were both surprised by the word "informal" on the invitation, but when we asked, we were told "That's Hollywood."]

STANTON: Or worse.

GALLEJAS: Going blind.

PETER: Dying.

GALLEJAS: Having a facial nerve cut, a lower lid pulled down, a red eye.
[*Shrugs.*]
These things happen in life.

LADY AITKEN: There's a greater chance with a double-layered lift, so I'm told, than with the standard lift of the lower half of the face.

GALLEJAS: Or a chemical peel with carbolic acid. Do you know of that?

LADY AITKEN: No.

GALLEJAS: Quite simple, really. Just paint phenol on the face. Cover it with adhesive tape. Leave it on for forty-eight hours. And your wrinkles are gone.

PETER: How long does a face-lift last?

GALLEJAS: With fat excision, six to seven years. Four to five for a temporal lift. Then you can always have another—though there is a limit.

LADY AITKEN: The face is never quite the same as when you first go in for surgery. The effects of gravity and aging and all the things we don't really understand are going on even during surgery—they never stop.

[MAIDS *and* BUTLER *enter. They are covered with blood.*]

GALLEJAS: What is it?

MAID: We don't know, sir.

[*A pause.* GALLEJAS *ponders.*]

GALLEJAS: You're covered with blood.

MAID: Yes, sir.

GALLEJAS: It looks as though someone has been murdered.

MAID: Yes, sir, it does.

[*Silence.* GALLEJAS *ponders.*]

GALLEJAS: Who screamed?

MAID: We don't know, sir.

[*Silence*]

GALLEJAS: Did you?

SECOND MAID: Not me, sir, no.

GALLEJAS: How did you come to be covered with blood?

FIRST MAID: The body was about waist high, lying on the table, when it began to spurt blood.

GALLEJAS: It began to spurt blood.

FIRST MAID: Yes, sir.

GALLEJAS: Had someone stuck it?

FIRST MAID: No, sir, I don't believe so.

GALLEJAS: How did it get on the table?

BUTLER: It had been stuffed in the dumbwaiter, sir.

GALLEJAS: From above or below?

BUTLER: I couldn't tell, sir.

GALLEJAS: How was it?

BUTLER: Bloated, sir. Belly distended. Pustules here and there. It was as we took it out of the dumbwaiter that its belly exploded.

LADY AITKEN: Poisoned?

BUTLER: Shot, madam, as near as I could tell.

LADY AITKEN: Was he a native?

BUTLER: Yes, madam.

GALLEJAS: It was a man, then.

BUTLER: Yes, sir.

GALLEJAS: A stranger shot elsewhere and then delivered to the premises.

BUTLER: So it would seem.

[*Silence*]

GALLEJAS: Why would someone do that?

BUTLER: I'm sure I don't know, sir.

GALLEJAS: What do you think?

BUTLER: I'm not entirely certain that I understand all the things that are and are not done, although I think I have acquired some knowledge of appropriateness, for instance, in a given situation: this ought to be postponed, this done at once, this calls for patience, this for dispatch, this for acquiescence, this for courage, and this, finally, for a certain manner of speaking which I think I can say fairly I have mastered. And of the forms of behavior, that a certain way of moving is not done, an attitude of the body, a certain footsound, a kind of glance, a manner of fixing one's ascot, a way of cocking the head, a certain presumption—all these are not done, whereas a kind of slam dancing is done, burning one's cheek with a cigarette is done, shooting out another's jaw is done, giving comfort to the grieving is not done, although you may think I am not one to judge, being a dependent person myself and yet on my day off I walk the streets, and as I cast my mind back over my own life I find more and more I remember less and less—I think it's fair to say I've come unhinged, having tried as I have to fit in and go along, after all, one needs to live, it can't be wrong to take a job, so that now as I look back I realize I have had twenty years of misery and could not say exactly who I am, for instance, or where my loyalties might lie at any given time, or what place I might call home, who my people are, these are things I think about on my day off when every week I go to a place where I sit in the front row, they do a striptease there, and after the show the same woman every week sits in my lap for a few minutes, and then in the park as I look around I see others quite like myself, sitting amidst the rubble, glass, and shattered stone, and I pray to Jesus—who else?—and I feel my mind is so filled with anguish as to have become a fire hazard—so that under the circumstances, sir, it seems to me that anything is possible. Would that be an answer to your question, sir?

GALLEJAS [*To a Maid*]: Have you anything to say?

[*Silence*]

MAID: No, sir.

[*Silence*]

STANTON: I don't mean to compare myself to a poet—really, not at all—but even bankers actually hope that what they are doing is, in a sense, creative. Building something. Bringing into being something that hadn't been there before. Structures that no one had seen before you made them, and not only do you make the structure but it results in physical, palpable things. A friend of mine, a banker, put together the money for the Alaska pipeline. Now whatever you think of that—and you always have to run cost-benefit analyses of these things—nonetheless he put together a structure of private and public capital—Citibank, Deutchesbank, underwriting companies, Morgan Stanley, Solomon Brothers. An impressive group, Lazard Freres, government agencies, an extraordinary act of imagination, really. Sometimes you can look at the financial plan that has been put together to finance a skyscraper, and the financial plan is a beautiful thing really by itself, a novel thing, very often an avant-garde thing, even a thrilling piece of intellectual daring, if you are sensitive to that sort of thing. And you look at the finished building and you actually see all these extraordinary structures of finance and political arrangements and mechanical stress and the molecular structure of the materials and you are moved by it. And there is something very powerful and captivating about a structure. You actually take some pride in what you are contributing to this society. You even think—though I know this is difficult for some people—that you have earned your income, or at least that it's not despicable to accept it, because this is the way society is structured and you are doing your part to keep it together and keep it going and make it a humane place.

GALLEJAS: Where is the body now?

BUTLER: It's gone, sir.

GALLEJAS: Gone?

BUTLER: Yes, sir.

GALLEJAS: Gone entirely, you mean.

MAID: Entirely, sir.

[*Long silence*]

GALLEJAS: Well, in that case, you may serve dessert.

MAID: Yes, sir.

[BUTLER *and* MAIDS *exit.*]

[*The sound of breathing—as though of someone asleep, with occasional sharp inhales and sobs, for a while.*]

MERIDEE [*Very quietly*]: I think we'd better leave.

PETER: Didn't we just get here?

MERIDEE: I don't think I feel well.

GALLEJAS: That's quite normal.

LADY AITKEN: I often feel that way myself. It passes soon enough.

PETER: She'll be all right.

STANTON: This is not a usual sort of thing.

MERIDEE: What have they done with it?

GALLEJAS: Thrown it out by the roadside, I expect.

MERIDEE: Thrown it out?

GALLEJAS: Did you want to see it?

MERIDEE: See a dead body?

GALLEJAS: Some people like it.

PETER: I understand that.

MERIDEE [*Still quietly*]: Let's get out of here.

PETER: We can't just leave.

STANTON: It's not easy.

LADY AITKEN: One can't leave one's friends. One has—associations.

STANTON: Obligations.

PETER: You get used to it.

LADY AITKEN: One's life becomes so—entwined. And where would one go? Who would one be somewhere else? I suppose one could say, really, we never should have come to begin with; but, then, we did. And here we are.

STANTON: One thing led to another.

LADY AITKEN: I don't know whether one thing led to another, but here we are. And it is awkward to leave. And what would you take?

MERIDEE: Take?

LADY AITKEN: I'd take my underwear, I imagine. Other things you can buy easily enough, but one always needs fresh underwear, and it's so hard to find on the road. When the Whitlaws left Africa, Annie Whitlaw neglected to take any underwear with her, and she was devastated. I often remember the little traveling case that Marie Antoinette had—a case of leather, with a silk lining, and filled with several dozen perfumes and creams, all in exquisite little silver jars and vials—and she kept it always prepared and ready to go. I always thought, you know, that she was rather an underrated person, knowing that all there was to do is wait.

STANTON: Why didn't she just leave?

LADY AITKEN: Why don't you leave?

PETER: Don't they bury their bodies here?

GALLEJAS: Not usually.

PETER: Are they that superstitious?

GALLEJAS: No, no. They'll be shot for it, you know.

[*Silence*]

PETER: No.
[*Beat*]
I didn't know. Is that why their villages smell so?

GALLEJAS: Do they?

PETER: When you drive through the countryside you get that dreadful odor coming in through the window. Like you get in Mexico sometimes. I always thought it was just the way they smell, you know, Mexicans. Sometimes you pass one on the street and they give off this smell, too, I'm not saying it's genetic or anything, but just, you know, well, let's face it, they, you know, have odor.

[*In moving lights:* And come to think of it, where would she go? And what would she do? And would that be tolerable now?]

LADY AITKEN: Oh, I'm afraid this conversation is going to get horribly boring. Mrs. Fish, I remember, once had all the guests at her luncheon talk baby talk to keep the conversation light. To be sure, sometimes one's mind just takes hold of something and there's no reining it in. I remember when Eleanor Roosevelt died, she insisted on a wooden coffin. She and Franklin had heard that if one were buried in a metal coffin, one's corpse would liquefy. They both meant to be buried in wooden coffins, but Franklin died at Warm Springs, and by the time Eleanor got there he had already been embalmed and put in a metal coffin, and the glass plate had been sealed, and it was spring, you know, and rather warm, and they had the train ride to take back to Washington, so she let it go, but it always bothered her to know that Franklin had just turned to ooze.

STANTON: It's a delicate matter, no doubt of it.

GALLEJAS: Here, the dogs get them. The jackals. The vultures. It's all quite natural.

[*A monkey screams.*]

STANTON: People don't think it of bankers, I suppose, but on the whole, actually, I never was the sort of fellow to believe: well, if I don't do it someone else
will. My father was a fine man, and I was raised with certain expectations, and
then I got into this business, and before I knew it, I thought: well, on the
whole, this is not so bad. And, after all, I'm not killing people.

[*Silence. His eyes fill with tears.*]

LADY AITKEN: Of course the important thing is to send the children home.
Howard and I have sent them home. One must be realistic. You don't keep
your children with you here.

GALLEJAS: No.

STANTON: Don't you miss them?

LADY AITKEN: Miss the children?
[*She tunes out, lost in thought.*]
We don't think about it.

HOWARD: We think about the children all the time! We never think of anything else! You spend your life reading them books, tucking them in, swimming, catching them off the edge of the pool, dressing them for birthday
parties, wearing funny little hats—God knows, you can't take enough pictures. All the time they're growing up, you take pictures, but you can never
take enough.

[*He is crying—the tears just coming quietly, from a man whose emotional
governors simply no longer function.*]

And you teach them to be decent, after all. You can't raise these children
without hope!

[*Silence. The others all look at him, turn away in discomfort.*]

STANTON: The oddest vision sprang to my mind not long ago about my son.
His face had been burned, a third-degree burn, and I'd taken him to a doctor
who said he would need certain treatments, certain face packs. And then I'd
just gone off to Mexico City and left my son for a week, and, when I got back,
it was too late to do anything for him.

PETER: But I mean, not everyone thinks of leaving. Some people have just started out, and hope they will have interesting careers—and they make no apology for it. They came here to pitch in, and they're ready to pitch in. I mean I am interested in opportunity. And have servants: I mean, people do think of these things, how nice it is. The servants here are really awfully nice people, and I mean you feel so well taken care of, and the beaches and the free time, and I mean, altogether there's just a terrific ease of living.

STANTON: No doubt.

PETER: What do you mean by that?

STANTON: No doubt. I mean: no doubt.

PETER [*Shouting*]: You mean you think I'm a son of a bitch. That's damned easy for you to say.

STANTON: Oh, I . . . no . . .

[*He falls back on his chair, his hand instinctively to his heart.*]

GALLEJAS: I must admit, I myself am rather fond of spinach frittata. I don't mind a bit of luxury. I am rather partial to the touch of silk, aren't you? I've seen all the films of Andrzej Wajda. Would you believe it of a provincial character like myself? I rather like the music of Philip Glass, do you? Of course, if you wish to have a high culture, you must have leisure; if you would have leisure, you must have excess wealth. If you would have excess wealth, you must exploit someone. And finally what is human life worth if it produces nothing of excellence, nothing of beauty, nothing extraordinary, nothing astonishing, if it only manages, day in and day out, to get along? Don't you find that somehow less than human?

LADY AITKEN: I believe in art. I think I would like to be a painting. Those of us who can't paint should be painted, I think.

[*In moving lights:* Could this be true?]

GALLEJAS: And, I must say: I'm not eager to give up my garden. My terrace. What would be the point? What do you think would happen? After the hedges are trampled, after the throats are cut, after the women are raped, after the bodies are mutilated, after the mass executions throughout the countryside?

[*Beat. With contempt.*]

Soon enough, you'd see a new bunch sitting here on the terrace. Possibly without tastes as fine as ours—these are barbarians, after all, after all these years they've been barbarized.

[*Beat*]

And what would they do, except that those among them with the finest instincts for bullying would rise to the top and society would be reconstituted exactly as it is today, with the most elusive scum among them moving from tax haven to tax haven in their private boats and planes and taking their women with them.

[*Beat. To Meridee.*]

You look at me as though I am some particular form of scum. But look what's happened to you: You've become my accomplice. I was born here, but you've come of your own free will! How utterly absurd! And now you wonder what you ought to do? Well, you ought to tear your hair out. You ought to weep and cry out and run through the streets dressed like a cockatoo!

HOWARD: How you start out. Who you think you are. Who you think you can become. What you learn. What you study. How you learn to think. Plato. What you believe. Descartes, Rousseau.

[*He begins to leak tears again.*]

You show you can do it. You prove you can do it. Then you begin to do it. If you didn't have children, if you didn't fear the bad example you would set, you'd kill yourself.

LADY AITKEN: You haven't done so badly, Howard.

HOWARD [*Casually—no longer having the energy to argue*]: Oh, well. Killing fourteen-year-old boys . . .

[*Silence*]

LADY AITKEN [*Putting it in a good light*]: Of course one always says, well, it's a matter of the reason, a matter of in this case or for this purpose or this time under these circumstances, whatever it may be, and then, before one quite knows it, it simply becomes:what one does!

HOWARD [*Again without much feeling*]: Shivs up their backsides.

LADY AITKEN: In the olden days, people studied the liberal arts, and conversations positively sparkled. What do people know any more but the warning signs of cancer, the rules of proper diet, the techniques of stress management, the knowledge of when to move money and of when to move?

HOWARD [*With sudden conviction and rage*]: We agreed in the beginning and I went out there. I did it. Now we are staying. I am not quitting. Because I am not quitting. And I make no apology for it!

[*Three scrims tear in half, one after another, and fall to the floor. A fourth scrim descends slowly, to cover the torn scrims, and is lit with a beautiful light.*

Music: Gentle, and beautiful, like a Salvadoran flute: piercing, melancholy, tragic]

VOICE-OVER: [*A soft, quiet, female voice, matter-of-fact, not seductive*]: I dreamed last night that I needed to change. I went into the women's room at the railroad station, into one of the stalls, and closed the door. I took off my raincoat and laid it on the floor, and then took off all my clothes and laid them carefully on the raincoat. And then the raincoat, with all the clothes on it, was drawn slowly out underneath the stall door—and I couldn't stop it, and all my clothes were gone, and I was left alone, and naked.

[*Projections: On one screen a movie, on the other stills. The stills are the sort of bedrooms one sees in* Town and Country *magazine; the films are very beautiful, slow motion, dreamy helicopters, exploding bombs, flames, smashing buildings.*

Projected words: I think everything is fantasy, really. What we surround ourselves with, how we relate to color, how we see beauty—it takes a long time to develop, but I've reached the point where everything is fantasy.]

PETER: I dreamed last night I was coming up the stone stairway at the market.

MERIDEE: Is this the story you told me?

PETER: Yes.

MERIDEE: And he saw this man who had been burned from head to foot.

PETER: He had no eyebrows, no eyelashes. He shivered convulsively. By the time I got to the top of the steps I was shaking with fear. And there was a woman who had been shocked speechless by the sight of the burned man. She grabbed me. She was already weak and dying. I pushed her. And she fell backwards, down the steps.

[*Pause*]

And as she fell, I thought: she would have died of her diseases anyway; it was almost an act of euthanasia to kill her. And that's how I feel. I feel that way.

[*The lights fade sickeningly, flicker, and resume with a dozen explosions of strobe flashes.*]

STANTON: I had the same dream.

LADY AITKEN: One is so fragile, after all.

STANTON: Sometimes it seems to me that my instincts are those of an insane person. They seem good to me and yet I feel entirely insane.

LADY AITKEN: Yes.

STANTON: I dreamed I came into a room filled with heads, waiting for relatives to come and claim them.

LADY AITKEN [*Dropping her glass*] Oh . . .
[*Beat*]
I'm sorry.

HOWARD: I was putting my son to bed one night, when the whole facade fell off the front of the house—just fell away into the street, and my son's bed was there, next to the edge. And I just told him to pull his bed back away from the edge, and I left him there, exposed to the night.

[*A horrendous, shattering explosion that rocks the theater. Music opens explosively.* MERIDEE *stands, in a panic, looks around with mounting anxiety, and, during the following moments, exits.*

THE ACTORS *sit and are served dessert by the servants.*

Projections: Beautiful things broken. Churches smashed. A broken tree. A shattered vase. A child's broken toy. A ruined bedstead. One picture, of a woman who has been hit in the mouth with a rifle butt, appears several times.

Sounds: Explosions. Hammering: as of hammer on stone, club on wood, fist on flesh. A high-pitched piercing sound. Terrible screams. The breaking of glass as though whole walls of glass are crashing down. The siren that the Nazis used. Helicopter blades, deafeningly. A babble of shouting, laughing, panicky directions, crowds in riot.

Voice-over: Toward the end, as the other sounds become intermittent, then fade, a soft, female voice reads a list of charity benefits for the month in Los Angeles.

The lights ease toward twilight. Howard remains in a brighter light.]

GALLEJAS [*To Peter. As they talk, their pictures are projected as at first. Their voices are miked to echo.*]: Do you shoot?

PETER: Certainly.

GALLEJAS: I go on a shoot from time to time in Baden-Baden.

PETER: Really?

GALLEJAS: I find it helps relieve the tedium. One can only take so much of buttermilk and cottage cheese and those wretched unsalted bits of waferbread before one wants to shoot something.

PETER: Yes.
[*A silence. He ingests the drug du jour.*]

I know it's wrong of me, but I've never enjoyed Baden-Baden. I like the massage, but I don't care for all that water and the deep breathing and calisthenics.
[*He thinks.*]
I don't mind a little brushing and scraping, having my pores cleansed, my torso packed in astringent gels, a pedicure, but I don't care for those sessions of lymph drainage.
[*Offering his drug to Gallejas*]
Have some?

GALLEJAS: Thanks.

[*Soundtrack: The sound of someone breathing, panting, as though running.*]

[*As they prepare and share drugs, their voices are heard over the loudspeaker, very smooth, quiet, almost whispering. The conversation drifts—long silences sometimes occur between remarks.*]

GALLEJAS'S VOICE: Life is more difficult but not impossible. I go out a lot—not to Paris much any more—but around here. I never really thought seriously of doing anything else.

LADY AITKEN'S VOICE: It's a natural, traditional pursuit—part of our heritage, and a recognized method of population control.

GALLEJAS'S VOICE: I don't know how many rooms there are. Somewhere around thirty-five or so, I've been told.

PETER'S VOICE: I guess I'd have to say the way I feel is: I don't have a problem with it.

LADY AITKEN'S VOICE: Sometimes I feel, you know, utterly transparent.

GALLEJAS'S VOICE: In my country, I see so little difference, generation to generation.

LADY AITKEN'S VOICE: There are still people who do it every day but it isn't what it used to be. People are wearing the wrong jackets and don't even know the rules.

[*The lights go to deep pinks and reds, the colors of sunset, lingeringly. The sound of the ocean and tropical birds. Three distinct, deliberate gunshots, coming almost from within the room. Startlingly present and real in sound. They should be fired by a pistol and not come over a loudspeaker. With the third one Howard's head suddenly explodes, and blood is splattered all over the rear wall. The lights fade slowly.*]

THE END

Orestes

Orestes, based on the play by Euripides, incorporates passages inspired by or taken from twentieth-century texts of Apollinaire, William Burroughs, Cindy, Bret Easton Ellis, John Wayne Gacy, Mai Lin, Elaine Scarry, Roberto Mangabeira Unger, *Vogue*, and *Soap Opera Digest*. The piece was developed in collaboration with Robert Woodruff, in a workshop he directed at the Mark Taper Forum in Los Angeles. Its earliest productions were directed by Tina Landau at the American Repertory Theatre in Cambridge, Massachusetts; by Robert Woodruff again at the University of California, San Diego; by Anne Bogart at the Saratoga International Theatre Institute in Toga, Japan, and Saratoga, New York; by Tina Landau again for En Garde Arts in New York; and by others.

Orestes

Characters

WILLIAM

JOHN

NOD

ORESTES

TAPEMOUTH MAN

THREE NURSES

ELECTRA

FORENSICS EXPERT

HELEN (and HERMIONE)

FARLEY

VOICES OVER THE RADIO

MENELAUS

MENELAUS'S BODYGUARD

TYNDAREUS

PYLADES

PHRYGIAN

APOLLO

Thrilling sounds of bombs, rockets, whistle flares, and other explosions and sonic marvels make the theater rock and shudder.

A green fog covers the stage, gradually clearing, and revealing a palatial white Newport-style or Palm Beach–style beach house whose façade we see, across a broad expanse of grass, from the oceanside. The lawn is ruined, with dug up sections of dirt and water.

And we hear a radio—as though it were the only thing still working in a back-yard in which all life had recently been annihilated—going on with the weather report, local traffic, news, and music.

*But the setting is both inside and out. Four very bright white hospital beds are set out on the lawn, in two of which are damaged war victims—*WILLIAM *and* JOHN*—who wear camouflage hospital gowns. They have occasional nightmares.* NOD, *similarly dressed, sits nearby in a wooden chair, his head hanging down.* ORESTES, *in one of the other beds, hands covered in dried blood, wears a red satin hospital gown. A man with tape over his mouth is tied up in a wheelchair. From time to time he is able to work free of the tape to speak.*

There are THREE NURSES *in attendance. They wear basic black.*

A yellow police-line tape surrounds the stage. The stage is lit with yellow tungsten parking lot lights. Overhead operating room lights hang over the beds.

Chair and table center stage. A radio is on the table. Microphones are scattered about.

It is six days after the murder of Clytemnestra.

ELECTRA *sits at the table, smoking a cigarette, drinking coffee. Her hands are covered in dried blood. She wears an Armani-designed pink ensemble, which she hasn't changed for a week.*

A FORENSICS EXPERT *in gray suit stands downstage, pointing to a cut-up female corpse on a steel autopsy slab.*

FORENSICS EXPERT: White female, age 38, presented to pathology with a slashed throat.

The subject was in good general health at the time of death. Approximately 5 feet 7 inches, 110 pounds. Skin unremarkable. Breasts small, no masses, everted nipples. Lungs clear to P and A. Abdomen sound—no masses.

We made a circular incision with a sharp razor around the umbilicus, deep enough to penetrate the skin, then from the middle of the pectoral bone a straight, lengthwise incision to the umbilicus, and from the lower region of the umbilicus as far as the region of the pubic bone between the little mounds of the vulva. We found no abdominal abnormalities or complications of the genito-urinary system.

The fatal wound to the neck was initiated with considerable force in the anterior and posterior triangles, in the levator scapulae and the scalene muscles and through the posterior belly of the digastric and the stylohyoid muscles. The blade proceeded through the carotid artery on the left side of the head and thence through the larynx and the vocal cords and on into the cervical vertebrae where the blade lodged and remained embedded.

Since the subject had presumably been in a warm bath, she hemorrhaged into the warm water and bled out rapidly.

The cause of death was heart failure.

ELECTRA [*Completely shattered and spent, having been awake for six days and nights drinking coffee and smoking cigarettes. Long silence as she stares off into space; then speaking as though for the hundredth time to a jury or to homicide detectives in a room at the stationhouse, way beyond exhaustion and control, or without any affect at all, taking her time—her job is to explain, make sense of it, make it cohere, and escape blame while accepting it.*]:

You could say:
"There is no form of anguish
however terrible
that human beings
might not have to bear."

Well.
There's a way of putting things in order.

You could say: my
my father Agamemnon was murdered by my mother
my mother Clytemnestra when he came back from the war.

And then my brother
Orestes: murdered our mother.

This was six days ago.

And now Orestes,
who would have been king,
lies huddled
there
in bed,
shivering, delirious, hallucinating.

[*The following item strikes her as pointless and stupid.*]

Martial law has been declared.

The people want to execute him for matricide—
and execute me with him,
as an accomplice.

Because:
I—encouraged him to do it.
I urged him to do it.

[*Offhandedly*]

It's a nightmare really.

Whose fault is this?
You could blame the gods for horror as absolute as this.
You could say:

[*Long silence; the exhaustion of going through the explanation again*]

this time, this country, these people

[*Exhausted—long silence*]

are somehow cursed.

You could say:

[*Abstractedly, as though the idea came from somewhere*]

they're held in some web of history and civilization
they can't untangle, even though
they made it with their own hands.

[*Silence*]

You could say:

[*Shrugs*]

it's politics.

[*Silence*]

You could say:

[*She begins to weep despite herself.*]

these two children:

[*Sobbing*]

it's all some dreadful abnormality from birth.
You could say:
look at the history of this family:

[*Laboring to explain, as though diagraming a sentence or a family tree*]

it depends on where you start you could say
Atreus—well, you could say Pelops murdered or:
Tantalus, you could start
Tantalus
the son of Zeus,
murdered his own son Pelops
to feed him to the gods.
To win the favor of the gods.
Fed his son to them.

[*Silence*]

Well, it's a common story.

Then, after Pelops was fed to the gods, his two sons,
Thyestes and Atreus,
fought with one another
and Atreus
killed the sons of Thyestes—
cooked them—
and served them for dinner to their father.

[*Lost a little in the bloodiness of this*]

What can be said about this?

[*Without interest in her conclusion, dismissing it as she says it*]

A certain need for position, a certain
homicidal rage
runs in this family.
The House of Atreus.

I think there are some things
that are close and distant at the same time:
Paradise for example.
The relations between a man and a woman.
The course a boat takes across the water.

When I travel I like the sort of luggage
where you can pack a metronome, or a piece of porcelain,
and know it will be safe.
And when it's snowing, I like to have a visitor.
A secret visitor.
And as you wait for him, you wonder: did he forget?

I don't know.
I don't remember.

So it's up to me to,
you know,
bring the family back together.

[*Still in the explanatory mode, but with tears welling up*]

The House of Atreus.
Atreus, by a second wife, had two sons:
my father Agamemnon,
and my uncle Menelaus.
And they married two sisters,
Agamemnon married Clytemnestra
and Menelaus married Helen
whose love affair was the cause . . .

[*Stops cold for a long time—looks off in space*]

or the occasion . . .
of the war in Troy.
Because

[*Struggling with this explanation, trying to remember how it goes*]

the two were brothers
—and they had married sisters—
the one had to help the other—
I don't know
it seemed so at the time
this was the reason that was given—

then it slips away
it happened very quickly.
Now our uncle Menelaus
comes home leading the soldiers
in a parade
to celebrate their victory.

[*With no affect at all*]

And my brother Orestes and I go to trial today
—before all the people—
to see whether we should be stoned to death or have our throats cut.
Only our uncle, the hero of the war against Troy, can save our lives.

[*Shrugs. Then, offhandedly*]

Our lives depend at last
on these people who brought us so much trouble,
on this
—man—
and on his "wife" Helen.

And here she is: unrepentant, untouched.

[HELEN *appears. She wears a canary yellow Chanel suit and carries flowers.*]

HELEN: First of all, I cleanse my skin with products that cleanse but don't dry,
products that are natural. I exfoliate my face once a week with a product that
contains oatmeal, honey, and nuts. The toner I use is alcohol-free, and I
moisturize all the time and use eye cream. I don't dry my skin out with products designed to clear up blemishes. This dries up your skin temporarily and
sends a message to your skin to produce more oil in that area, so it just makes
the problem worse. So I cleanse, tone, moisturize, and exfoliate. And I drink a
lot of water. And I relax. I find time to meditate, put my feet up and do a
facial mask and just think about the great powers of the universe and all that
we have to be happy about and grateful for.

But Electra, my dear, here you are.
I can't believe you murdered your own mother.

How appalling.
And you're still not married, a girl your age.
Of course you've had—distractions.
And your poor dear brother, how is he?

ELECTRA [*Disinterested*]: He's here.

HELEN [*Turning to see Orestes*]: Oh, my.
How sad.

[*Silence*]

Of course, you're not to blame.
You're only children.
One blames the gods for this sort of thing.
It's up to them.
I blame Apollo.

NOD: Some people say murder is a terrible thing, but then you hear of other things that make you think murder is a blessing.

JOHN: Sometimes the worst thing is just to be blindfolded for days on end waiting for someone to tell you why you're there. And then when they whip the blindfold off to question you, you're almost blind, the light is painful.

NOD: I know a man who spent twenty-seven months like that. No one else knew what he was held for.

JOHN: Or they will bring you in, five or six men, and say: this is nothing but the introductory exercise, and they will burn you with cigarettes.

NOD: And then, of course, if they have your wife, too, they will fondle her hair, whatever they want, while you watch. Just to show you they can do any-thing they want.

JOHN: Or they can nail you to some boards, put electric shocks to your tongue and ears and penis, and you find you wake up in a pool of cold water and they start in again.

NOD: Or sometimes they'll use drugs to induce delusions or make you writhe, you faint and fall down and hit your head on the walls and floor.

JOHN: It's a nightmare, really.

HELEN: But Electra, dear, could I ask you a favor?

ELECTRA: Ask me a favor?

HELEN: Will you go for me to my sister's grave?

ELECTRA: My mother's grave?

HELEN: To take an offering of hair and a libation from me.

ELECTRA: I couldn't bear to see my mother's grave.

HELEN: Well, I can't go. I couldn't bear to show my face in Argos.

ELECTRA: Why not?

HELEN: For fear.

ELECTRA: Fear

HELEN: And shame.

ELECTRA: Fear and shame.

[*Beat*]

Right. These are things you feel.

HELEN: Well, of course I do.

[*This catches Electra's attention; for a moment she comes awake.*]

ELECTRA: Well, of course you do.
But then you've had such—distractions.
Your life abroad.

The vexations of the war.
Of course you're not to blame
You were only children.
I blame Apollo.

HELEN: Apollo?

ELECTRA: What could you have done?

HELEN: So, yes, well,
so you understand?
I couldn't go.

ELECTRA: No.
Then send your daughter Hermione.

HELEN: Send a child?

ELECTRA: Who else?
It always seems to me there's something special
between a mother and her daughter.

HELEN [*Beat. Uncertain*]: Yes.

[*Beat. Makes up her mind*]

You're right. I'll send Hermione.

[*Calling out*]

Hermione, dear, come to me, dear.

[*A nurse brings out Hermione, who is a doll on a tricycle. She wears a white, floral Betsy Johnson sundress with matching leggings.*]

Hermione, dear, do just as I say.

Take these clippings of my hair and this libation of honey, milk, and wine and go to my sister Clytemnestra's grave. Stand right upon the heaped-up grave and say these words:

"Helen, your sister, sends these libations as her gift, fearing herself to approach your grave, from terror of the mob," and beg her not to harbor unkind thoughts toward me and my husband.

[*Beat. An afterthought*]

Or toward these two suffering children, who really can't be blamed either.

Do you understand?

HELEN [*In Hermione's voice*]: Yes, Mommy.

HELEN: There's a good girl. Go quickly now. Don't dawdle.

[*Hermione exits.*]

HELEN [*In Hermione's voice*]: Yes, Mommy.

HELEN: And come right back.

The world has become more difficult nowadays, not as it was when I was a child.

Of course, nonetheless,

[*She straightens things in her purse.*]

in the mornings I try to say nice things to myself, about myself, take better care of myself. And I get my eyelashes dyed—that helps—my eyebrows waxed, get a facial and get my hair done, and then I go out to lunch.

[*She is gone.*]

ELECTRA: God, how vile human nature is.

NOD: Sometimes I myself have a hunger just to let someone have it. I look around; I say: boy he really let him have it. Gee, he really got one off. And I'd like to get one off, you know, fast or slow, I don't give a fuck.

JOHN: Sometimes you can take a man apart in a few hours. You know, like you can win a whole war in the first three hours, although it may take some days or weeks for the other guy to know he's lost it. You can just beat a man on his shoulders for two or three hours and he's really come apart even though he doesn't know it yet.

NOD: Or sometimes you can take a woman, spend a little time with her, and send her away with a lot of pain in her breasts and wrists and ankles. Their genitals will become inflamed two, four months later; she'll start crying for no reason at all. And I have to admit, that makes me feel better.

[*The nurses enter, fixing the beds and ministering to the victims.*]

ELECTRA [*Going protectively to Orestes' bedside*]: Please. Don't disturb my brother.

NURSE 1: Don't worry, dear. We won't touch him.

ELECTRA: Let him sleep.

NURSE 3: We'll let him sleep, dear.

ELECTRA: If you wake him up, you know, he could wake up dead.

NURSE 3: No, no, no. He'll be all right.

NURSE 2 [*Under her breath, to Nurse 1*]: Where did she get that idea?

ELECTRA: There are certain people who, in earlier times we might think: well, these people are confused, they can't make up their own minds in a healthy way, we must stop them. Now, we think: no, if that's their way of thinking, what right have we to say ours is superior? We may think they are confused, but they have the facts as we do and they have their own way of reasoning, and they have to live with themselves, so it's up to them, really. The same thing with euthanasia: we say, well, if a person is suffering and would rather be released from the suffering, that seems only right.

And, take for instance the example of a person suffering but in a coma, a person who would decide on suicide if he or she were fully conscious, and if life in the future is going to be nothing but suffering: well, then, we say, the family ought to be able to make the decision for that person, to put her out of her suffering. We all accept that now, and I can see why. Or, take hookers. We all think that's a terrible thing to do, from our own point of view, but there's nothing less terrible, really, about putting your mind at someone else's service, even, when you think of it, it might be worse, but you can't despise it if that's what she has to use, you know, and not even for necessities, really, but even if she wants to use it for getting some luxuries or pleasures or comforts. And I can see the point of view of terrorists, too. I don't happen to think you can say terrorists are all bad or that their actions aren't, really, in some sense, a form of political expression, who are suffering enormously and have no alternative, no way to get what they want, usually, and it seems to me that they are really, though they may not quite know it, in the same position as the terminal cancer patient, that if they were fully conscious that they would recognize that, and that since they aren't fully conscious, we ought really to make that decision for them, just as we do for others who are in pain, because these people are in pain, this is something I know, because I've felt pain myself all these years, and I know how they feel. And they ought to be put out of their suffering.

[*Orestes wakes with a cry. All the other victims are startled awake and freak out, and then subside.*

This next scene between Orestes and Electra, is more than one of love between siblings; it is romantic. But it is also archaic; this is a ruined fragment of the Greek play in the midst of the modern world.]

ORESTES [*Quietly now, speaking each word as though it were a palpable object*]: Oh, sweet sleep.
Sweet savior of the sick.
How good it was to sleep. How I: needed it.

[*Silence*]

How wise the gods are,
if they give us life,
to give us sleep.

ELECTRA: Orestes.

ORESTES: Electra, oh
my
sister.
Where are we now?

ELECTRA: Shall I lift you up?

ORESTES: Just hold me.

[*She does.*]

ELECTRA: Shall I brush the hair from your eyes?

ORESTES: Yes, and—
my lips—
are dry.
What is this at my lips?
Is this foam at my lips?
How disgusting sick people are.
Can I sit up?
Yes.

[*Looking around, wrapped in his sheet*]

Here we are, then.
I don't remember.
How hard it is to wake up, and wish you were asleep.

ELECTRA: Orestes, listen. There is hope for us.
Menelaus has just come back from Troy.

ORESTES: He could save us.

ELECTRA: Yes.

[*Suddenly, explosively, Orestes freaks out, shrieking—which freaks out everyone else in their beds and they, too, yell out.*]

ORESTES: No, you fuck! You fuck!
[*Trying to get something off his shoulder*]
Get these cocksuckers off me, I'll fuck you up,
you bitch!

ELECTRA: Orestes!

[*She tries to hold him down.*]

ORESTES: Let me go!

[*Speaking in a rush, in the voices he has heard of nurses or doctors*]

What's that behind that crazy talk? What terrible thing have you been thinking. Sick men should stay in bed!

[*She slaps him; he stops.*]

ELECTRA: It's nothing, Orestes!

ORESTES: No.
Right.
Thank you.

[*He leans back against the headboard, still in a daze.*]

Or you could say, for example, I did love her, I did love her, and I knew she loved me, even though she was in a sense you know anorexic and blond, that kind of girl, with creamy skin, pure, that kind of thing so that in the bedroom on her mattress in the dark, the candles burning out one by one, listening to music and stone drunk, you know and passed out, wasted, really, face it, I couldn't wait, I couldn't wait to get back to my own place so I finished her off fast, you know, she's chewing my lips and panting and her hair is all wet I'm thinking this is a witch, this is a witch, I hate these fucking people with their faces all twisted like they've gone totally insane you find yourself hacking at them, hacking at them with the butt of your hand, she says to me, you're seeing someone else, I said I am not, this is a fucking lie, that's not true at all, she says swear it, I said I do, she said you're fucking lying, you can't use the bathroom, and it's dark, it's freezing out, the fucking car won't start, the cigarette lighter is broken, that's when I slam the butt of my hand into the dashboard, I say goddam you fucker goddam you fucker and she reaches over and touches my leg, that was her mistake, I saw it, just my forearm I saw it moving through the air but it was too late then, so I pushed her out behind the diner with the garbage cans, it seemed a good place at the time.

[*The archaic style is restored.*]

ELECTRA: There's nothing here, Orestes.

ORESTES: No, it's just: my mind goes off from time to time.

[ELECTRA, *with the help of the* NURSES, *eases him back down; he lies back,
breathing heavily.*]

ELECTRA: Oh, God, is he going to be helpless now until they come to kill us?

[*Her eyes fill with tears.*]

ORESTES: What's the trouble?

ELECTRA: These are nothing but—shadows in your mind, Orestes. They'll go
away.

ORESTES: Yes.

ELECTRA: I'm sorry, Orestes.
Here you are like this because of me.
I think of nothing now but if I could just save you,
my brother.
I'm the one to blame.
I don't care.
There's nothing to be done.
If only I could save you, Orestes,
that's all I'd want.

ORESTES: No. No.
You talked about it,
but I committed murder.
That much is clear.
So much is gone—
or things I didn't see—
but there are moments cut—incised in my mind—
my mother's eyes, so lost.
A servant's scream.
My mother's eyes . . .
And what was the point?
I can't remember.

Our father is dead still.
And now, over and over,
the thought keeps coming back to me:
if I had asked my father
what it is I should have done
he would have told me
not to harm our mother.
Now there is nothing that can redeem what we have made of our lives.

But never mind.
Don't cry.
We'll help each other.
I don't blame you.
I wish you'd never spoken to me.
But I don't blame you.
I don't know.
It's a nightmare really.
It's in our blood.
We've been so close to one another since we were born,
all our lives.
But you should go,
you need your rest.
Just stay with me.

My sister.

[*He sinks back on his pillow delirious; he will be delirious through to the end of the play, white-faced, dizzy, ill and perspiring.*]

Ladies should never fall in love.
They become stars
no one can ever reach. To look taller
they cut their heads off and stand on them.

They carry their breasts
in gunny sacks
and unbutton their nerves at night
in front of vibrators
staring at pictures
of bearded men.

Some fall in love with foreign accents
and dark vowels.
You see them late at night
in taverns, talking with dangerous criminals.
Late at night, their voices
are small animals
waiting to be fed

[*He closes his eyes.*]

ELECTRA: I could never leave you, Orestes.
We're bound together now
as we never were.
I wouldn't have it any other way.

[*The phone rings*]

ELECTRA: Hello?

FARLEY [*Voice-over*]: Electra, is this you?

ELECTRA: Yes.
[*Beat*]
Farley?

FARLEY: Yes!

ELECTRA: I was hoping you would call. I've been thinking about what you
said. And I'd just like you to explain about conjunctions a little more, because
I think I'm having some kind of trouble with mine.

FARLEY: Well, if you have too many conjunctions in your natal chart, as I
think you do—is that right?—

ELECTRA: Yes.

FARLEY: Right. Well, then you often live with a fog or a veil. Remember the
basics: a conjunction is where two planets come very close together in the sky.
For example, conjunctions with Mars or Saturn can be very painful and con-
fusing, especially if these two planets themselves are conjunct.

ELECTRA: I see.
Farley?

FARLEY: Yes.

ELECTRA: Farley?

FARLEY: Yes.

ELECTRA: Can I ask you a question?

FARLEY: Sure. Go ahead.

ELECTRA [*Fearfully*]: What if I had Jupiter in my natal conjunction. You know, would that mean something about my mother?

FARLEY: Wow. Well, there you would be adding expansion, philosophy, travel, and foreigners to the mix. So, oftentimes if you add Jupiter you'll be pushing the panic button on the other planets, because of the expansion aspect, you know you could be pushing the button on sex or whatever. Or say you have Jupiter conjunct with Mars, you'd be in for some very heavy duty macho aggressive or hostile stuff. Because astrology is a science of combination. See what I mean?

ELECTRA: Yes. Thank you, Farley.

FARLEY: OK!

[*She hangs up, starts to leave.*]

ORESTES: Electra?

ELECTRA: You rest. I'm right here.

[*Sits back down and after a moment speaks distractedly—at first as though consoling Orestes, then to herself.*]

I think that what happens is that we are put in places and situations in time, either Cleopatra on her barge, or someone in the galley rowing the barge, or out in New Guinea or in a space colony. We know where we're going, or we feel it, so it's not something we dwell on.

There was a time I might have had a life of many choices. You might say: well, what choice do you have? Being a woman of a certain position and so forth, so much seems given. And yet some people do have the privilege, the wealth, all those things to do anything they want to do. You think, well: if you had been born in some other country, under other circumstances, you might say you had no choice. But you, let's face it, the life you have will be the life you make.

And then you think: can this be true? This is not what I had in mind at all. Or at least I didn't think I did.

[*Orestes is asleep; she exits. The* NURSES *play mah jong. One of them hums a lullaby-like song. They speak an occasional phrase over the game. One of them turns on a radio, and we hear a warm, quiet voice on a radio talk show.*]

RADIO VOICE: I think sometimes
how nice it would be
to go someplace like Sulawesi . . .

OTHER RADIO VOICE: Right.

RADIO VOICE: and spend some time among the orchids
have drinks brought up by native women
or drive along the country roads, past the goats,
and spend some time on the beach.

OTHER RADIO VOICE: Unh-hunh.

RADIO VOICE: People say they have good surf,
and the natives on the seashore are always so much more easygoing—
that's what they always say.
You could spend some time fishing off a charter boat,
look at the boutiques, the bars and dive shops,

OTHER RADIO VOICE: Right.

RADIO VOICE: shop in their markets for peppers,
see the local farmers with their machetes stuck in their belts,
their daughters working at the cheese press.

OTHER RADIO VOICE: Yes, I know just what you mean.

RADIO VOICE: I like an airy room, where you can hear the roar of the surf,
get a nice burn by day,
cool off at night.

This is the reward of hard work, after all;
if you can't enjoy the pleasures that you've earned,
what's the point of earning them at all?

[*An explosion of static and then cheers and applause over the radio, and another
radio or hand-held amplified bullhorn cuts over the first.*]

But here he is now, just coming into sight, Prince Menelaus, who returned
from Troy last night and entered the city this morning.

[*Enormous cheers and a riot of static.* MENELAUS *enters. A man in a trenchcoat
enters with him, stands at a distance, moves occasionally to be not too distant
from him. Once again, there is a formality here, an archaic manner that is a
remnant of the Classical world.*]

MENELAUS: Thank you.
We're happy to be home.
Happy to be home.
Helen and I had a pleasant journey home.
And I couldn't be happier to be here.
And, at the same time: sad, of course.
The news of Agamemnon's death reached us on our journey back.

TAPEMOUTH MAN [*Having worked free of the tape.*]: Pedaios, son of Antenor,
struck with a spear behind the head at the tendon, piercing straight on
through the teeth and under the tongue, cutting off the power of speech
learned at the knee of Theano who reared him carefully even as her own children;

Phereclus, son of Harmonides the smith, struck in the right buttock, the
spearhead passing through the bone and into the bladder so that he dropped,
screaming, to his knees, taking with him his father's knowledge of how to
fashion intricate things with his hands;

Robert Gilray, dropped by artillery fire coming from the left, entering his body and beginning there its dark explosion, obliterating the standing crowd that each week watched his swift run across the playing fields of Chatham;

Manuel Font, around whose fragile frame the fire closed in, burning into his skin, skull and brain, even into the shy corners where he studied at school; shells and missiles, unmaking the terrain where pianos could be played and bicycles could be pedaled, unmaking customs, manners, knowledge, class-mates, comrades, schools . . .

MENELAUS: Who is this?

[*A* NURSE *slaps the Tapemouth Man, stopping him, and she puts the tape back over his mouth with the help of the trenchcoated man.*]

MENELAUS: But where is our nephew Orestes?
We've come to comfort him.

ORESTES: Here I am, uncle.

[*He lurches from bed, staggers forward toward Menelaus.*]

But first, before I tell you what I know let me hear you say you'll save us. She did nothing wrong, and I . . . I was driven to it by demons I don't understand.

[*He falls at Menelaus's feet, grabs one of his feet, which Menelaus gently tries to extract.*]

MENELAUS [*Involuntarily, under his breath*]: What a disgusting sight.

ORESTES: Oh, uncle.
Is my appearance offensive to you?

MENELAUS: Well: you look like death.
That matted hair. Those filthy clothes.
What's this on your hands? Is it blood?

ORESTES: We are blood relatives, you and I.
And each of us, in our way,

is responsible for spilling some.
Are your hands clean?

[*Takes Menelaus's hands and turns them over.*]

Don't let looks deceive you.
We are soulmates you and I.
At home and abroad.
And this is how a man looks these days if his
conscience is still alive.

MENELAUS: This is not at all what I'd . . .

ORESTES: I'm sinking deeper and deeper into a world of remorse and
madness. There's no bottom to this.

MENELAUS: Of course there is. What nonsense. When did this come on?

ORESTES: I was at my mother's grave.
I put a handful of dirt on her fresh grave.
And all at once I was surrounded by these phantoms.
Three women, black as night.

MENELAUS [*Stopping Orestes*]: That's enough.

NOD: Sluts!

MENELAUS: What's this?

JOHN: The sluts!

MENELAUS: Who are these people?

ORESTES: These are my fellows. You may speak in front of them just as you
would speak to me in private.

MENELAUS: So these Furies pursue you. Well and good.
But how do you stand with the people?

ORESTES: They shun me.

MENELAUS: Who are your worst enemies?

ORESTES: Everyone.

MENELAUS: What's their plan? Have they a plan?

ORESTES: They vote today to sentence us.

MENELAUS: Either banishment or death.

ORESTES: They've ruled out banishment.
They vote whether to stone us or cut our throats.

MENELAUS: Things have gotten far along.
You should run.

ORESTES: The city is surrounded by armed men.

MENELAUS: Armed men. How many?

ORESTES: Enough to ring the city.

MENELAUS: A private army?

ORESTES: No. All the citizens of the city, all armed.

MENELAUS: I see. They're all against you.

ORESTES: I don't feel well. A little dizzy.

NURSE 1: Here comes Tyndareus, all dressed in black,

NURSE 3: in mourning for his daughter Clytemnestra.

ORESTES: Oh, no, this is the end for me.
My grandfather, in a rage.
My grandfather, who once considered me his favorite.
Now wants me dead.

[TYNDAREUS *enters.*]

TYNDAREUS: Oh, is this boy here?
I hadn't supposed you kept company with matricides, Menelaus.:
How very liberal-minded of you.

MENELAUS: He is my kin.

TYNDAREUS: He was my kin, too.
And loyalty is to be admired to a point.
But blood ties are broken when a boy spills his mother's blood,
even if that mother was herself a barracuda.
Draw distinctions, Menelaus. Make judgments.

MENELAUS: These things are never quite so simple.

TYNDAREUS: Oh, yes, they are.
One doesn't try to govern another man's imagination,
another man's emotions,
another man's personal preferences,
idiosyncrasies, indulgences, passions, tastes, whims,
so long as they do no harm to the bodies of others;
but, as for actions,
these we govern all the time, and should.
This is what it is to be a man,
and nothing else.

ORESTES: Grandfather, if you would speak to me . . .

TYNDAREUS [*To Orestes*]: If I would speak to you, how should I speak?

I know one mustn't use certain expressions these days,
among your generation.
One mustn't call people barracudas, for example
no matter how they behave.

Shall I apologize?
This was your mother, after all,
my daughter,
even if she was a slut.

But one mustn't speak this way, I know.
For this is rude and might offend one's feelings.

[*He takes his time.*]

There are words these days, I know, that cause a certain pain—like "slut" or "sweetie" or "dear" or "peg leg," or—"watermelon."

There is some quality of magical thinking in this, a certain primitive turn of mind, if I may use the word, that seems to fly to the belief that if one disposes of a word, one disposes of all the dreadful or disagreeable things that have become attached to it.

So that if one simply doesn't use the word "articulate," in referring to a certain sort of person, as though a certain sort of person's competence with language were an exceptional matter, then the exceptionality of this articulateness will disappear.

Or, if one will eschew the word "community," in speaking of a group of people, as though that group shared a monolithic culture in which they all acted and thought in the same way, then one's language would not create ghettoes in which these groups are constrained to live. One should never refer to the black community, for example, or the gay community. One should refer, rather, to the black residents in a southside neighborhood.

Then, too, one ought not say "oreo" in reference to black Americans who have abandoned their culture, or refer in a similar fashion to Asians as bananas or Mexicans as coconuts.

One ought not say "illegal alien," when one has available such vocabulary as "undocumented worker" or "undocumented resident."

One ought not use the expression "qualified minorities," as though minorities were in general unqualified.

One ought not use the word "swarthy."

One ought not say "blond and blue-eyed" unless one is prepared to use the expression "brown-haired and brown-eyed" as an expression of equal attractiveness.

One ought not say "inscrutable" in speaking of an Asian.

One ought not say "Dutch treat," as though to say the Dutch people are cheap.

One ought not say "fried chicken," under any circumstances as I understand it.

One ought not say "Jew"—or I should say that some people prefer the expression "Jewish person," and in any case that the word should never be used as a synonym for stingy. And that it should always be used as a noun, never as a verb.

One ought not say "buxom" or "fragile" or "feminine" or "pert" or "petite" or "gorgeous" or "stunning" or "statuesque" or "full-figured" or in any other way refer to the physical attributes of a woman.

I can accept all this with equanimity.

And yet, one can commit murder and find the words to justify it.

This is your sort of civilization, then. It speaks nicely and behaves barbarously.

Indeed, it thinks that speaking well, putting a nice face on things, will transform the very stuff of life on earth.

No, no, no.
You've come unhinged.
You've lost your bearings altogether.
You've assaulted the very foundations of your home.
You've forgotten who you are, where you come from.

You remember nothing: not your parents, nor the values they held dear, not your country, nor the polity it once held in its grasp, or at the very least aspired to, not your history, nor your religion, nor even the most rudimentary tenets of ethics or gentleness.

And this is what you ask me to give my blessing to.
No.

[*To Menelaus*]

As for you, Menelaus, I don't expect some form of civil behavior from a man who has just returned from rendering an entire civilization a smoking ruin, while his own home sinks in rot and violence, husbands murdered by their wives, mothers murdered by their sons, sleeping children shot through bedroom doors. I know of a boy who poured kerosene on a derelict and lit him on fire and burned him to a crisp, not thinking he, the boy, had done anything wrong. That's the value they place on human life in the world that boy comes from. And soon enough such boys will fill your neighborhood. You flatter yourself that you are an old-fashioned sort of man, but you've no idea what it is you ought to be old-fashioned about.

And I will tell you this:
for the murder of my daughter,
I expect the murderer to suffer the punishment of the state.
No more. No less.
That's what I mean by a civil society.
I'll hold you responsible.
Let us begin there to put the world to rights.

[*Tyndareus leaves.*]

ORESTES: This is a hard man, my grandfather.

MENELAUS: Upright.

ORESTES: Hard.

MENELAUS: Strict.

ORESTES: But what could I have done? It's not so simple, as you say.

I killed my mother. But, from a certain point of view, this is no crime at all, since I was duty bound to avenge my father, to whom my mother had been unfaithful when he was fighting for our country. Was her wrong meant to go unpunished? If all women thought they could get away with murder, where would we be then? Are we to live from now on in fear of our own wives, no longer safe in our own homes?

You might say, I should have appealed to the civil authorities. But where are the civil authorities? To tell the truth, civil society lies in ruins.

[*Throwing in every argument he can think of: sick, frantic, over the edge, mopping his brow of perspiration*]

I've sent out a warning. I've set a precedent. In a certain sense, I should be rewarded. I've done a service to my country, just as you have, Menelaus, by going to war against Troy. It is exactly the same. Exactly. When the law will not come to their rescue, when there are others so reckless or unscrupulous or evil that they disregard all law and all ethical restraint, then men do their duty. That's what it is to be a man. Not to be paralyzed and disarmed by the complexity of all human affairs, but to work through a thicket of moral ambiguity, and then, with all due humility about the rectitude of one's own acts, nonetheless, to act.

Or else the world is left to sink of the weight of its own uncertainties.

Wallowing in crimes that go unpunished,
sucked down by wrongs left unresolved,
adrift in a world that feels sick
because no one can decide what should be done
or whether what it is that can be done
exceeds the cost of doing nothing.
I should be forgiven and rewarded for what I've done.

MENELAUS: Orestes, my son,
count on me.
Because for you, personally,
I have such a high regard.
And also because I recognize it is my duty
to lend a hand to any kinsman who's in trouble—
if the gods provide the means.

I only wish I had armed men at my disposal,
to move in forthrightly with a show of force—
not use it, mind you,
necessarily,
but show it—
and put an end to this.

As it is,
unfortunately,

as you know,
I've returned with my followers exhausted by their ordeal—
to find, in fact,
I'm not so popular even here at home.

And so,
I think it's clear,
to imagine we might rely on force,
or even an appearance of force,
would only be illusory.

But, in any case, in a situation like this, I've often found,
one much prefers to rely on suasion.
The power of the word:
never underestimate it.
And of patience.
Of letting things just take their course.
Of tact, and a sense of timing.

Because, when the people get swept away by some passion or other,
they're like children.
It is often hard to get their attention,
let alone to change their minds.

But if you just let them get it out of their systems,
it passes like a summer storm—
and soon enough
they don't even remember what it was that so upset them.

This is the civil way.

The skilled public man,
like the skilled sailor,
trims his sails in a strong wind,
and wins more by yielding than he ever can by force.

One must be attentive, of course.

Put in the right words where it counts,
when it will do the most good,

as I certainly will do for you.
This is nothing that a little skillful politicking cannot put to rights.

[*He gathers himself to exit.*]

Shore things up.
Have some feel for the shifting mood,
what people need,
what sorts of things they'll frankly trade,
what's important to them and what isn't,
what price they put on loyalty,

[*He begins to walk out, talking.*]

whether they demand it
or can demand it
or let it slide and miss their opportunity.
Give shape and purpose to the formless urges of one's countrymen.

This sort of thing is second nature to a statesman,
but we all can learn from the behavior of those we see in the public eye,
their lives may seem remote sometimes,
even as though their behavior had nothing to do with us,
and yet,
if we watch them closely
we sometimes learn a thing or two.

[*He's gone.*]

ORESTES: Slime!

WILLIAM [*Rising in his bed, speaking for the first time*]: One time I looked
through a telescope and saw the words: "two of each of anything, one facing
toward the other, put up as mirror images, to mark and mock a terminus."

This sign I saw by the edge of a brown lake lit by carbide lanterns, and in
the shallows of the lake I could make out a crablike fish that stirred the surface now and then and released some bubbles that bore up the stagnant smell
of swamp.

This was a soldier's camp.

One of them stepped forward and handed me an old Webley .455.

We were standing in front of what seemed to be an old abandoned barracks.
They lived there permanently, these soldiers,
guarding a shack surrounded by razor wire.
They welcomed me, opening a path right through the wire,
unlocking the door of the small cabin.
As I filed in through the door with them
a terrible stench, of some unknown origin,
filled our lungs.
I was overcome with nausea,
and the captain said to me:
welcome home.
It's a nightmare, really.

[*The phone rings; Orestes answers it.*]

ORESTES: Hello?

FARLEY: Hello?

ORESTES: Hello.

FARLEY: Hello, Orestes.

ORESTES: Yes.

FARLEY: This is Farley.
I know your sister.
I've talked to you before.

ORESTES: Yes.
Yes. I'm not feeling well.

FARLEY: Do you wish I wouldn't bother you?

ORESTES: No, no. I'm glad to talk to you.

FARLEY: I thought you might be thinking of making a decision—in fact, of taking an action.

ORESTES: Yes, in fact I was.

FARLEY: Well, I might have some advice for you.

ORESTES: Well, do you?

FARLEY: Yes. I do. You know, we're about to enter into a moon wobble, and I always tell people, if you plan on undertaking anything new of a major sort—not just daily living, buying and selling that kind of thing—but if you're thinking of buying a new home, buying a car, any new business, any new enterprise, this is something you definitely ought to do before a moon wobble, because, you will hear people tell you that you get a 10 to 15 percent disappointment rate for new projects during a moon wobble, but in my experience some people get up to a 50 to 70 percent disappointment rate. Do you know what falling in love can do when it happens in the middle of a moon wobble?

ORESTES: No.

FARLEY: Well, I don't recommend it. These are very, very karmic times. Do you want to test the universe? I don't think so. So I advise people to act before the wobble occurs. So, if I were you, I'd act before the end of the month. Okay?

ORESTES: Right.
Right. Thanks for your advice.

[*He hangs up. Pylades enters. He wears cobalt blue, Jean-Paul Gautier suit with silver threads, powder blue shirt, and a hand-painted silk tie. His hair is slicked back. He wears an earring and smokes Gitanes cigarettes.*]

PYLADES: Orestes. My friend. What's happening?
I saw the crowds coming through the streets.

ORESTES [*Hyped up, speeding.*]: It's over. Menelaus has stabbed me in the back.

PYLADES: You talked?

ORESTES: Yes, I'd better run for it now.

PYLADES: Did you talk to him?

ORESTES [*Angrily*]: Yes. Patience—caution—rot.
I don't remember.
And that bitch Helen is in my house.
I don't know.
And then Tyndareus.

PYLADES: He was angry.

ORESTES: Right.

PYLADES: Refused to help.

ORESTES: I don't know.

PYLADES: Well, as matters stand—

ORESTES: I don't remember.

PYLADES: the city under siege.

ORESTES: Right.

PYLADES: Armed men

ORESTES: Right.

PYLADES: in all the streets.

ORESTES [*Impatiently*]: Yes!

[*Silence*]

PYLADES: We're surrounded.

ORESTES: Well, I'm surrounded.

PYLADES: Well.
I'm ruined, too,
really.

ORESTES: What?

PYLADES: My father threw me out.

ORESTES: For what?

PYLADES: Aiding and abetting you.

ORESTES [*Beat*]: I'm sorry.
You should run for it.

PYLADES: I'm not a runner.
And, you know:
I wouldn't leave you now.

ORESTES: I never meant to drag you in.

PYLADES: Drag me, Orestes. Drag me.
I'm in it with you.
I'm your friend.
I always thought: spending time with you.
Getting to know some good people.
[*A smile and a shrug*]
Let's face it.
We've shared some friends.
Women.
Not that I'd do anything, you know.
Not that I'd swallow blood.
Not that I'd make candles out of human fat.
Not that I'd suck the juices from a corpse.
Not that I'd stick my tongue in an old man's anus.
Not that I'd cut off a man's cock and let it grow out my ass.

But, we have a history together.
You know.

[*We hear a song.* ELECTRA *appears upstage wearing what seems to be an old cocktail dress of Helen's. They are silent for a moment and then, throughout the following dialogue, Electra sings.*]

ORESTES: Yes, well, the time has come to run.

PYLADES: I thought you were the kind of person
who would never run.
And leave Electra behind?
Not even speak in your own defense.

ORESTES: Depend on the system of justice, you mean.

PYLADES: People from a certain sort of privilege . . .

ORESTES: Must be immune.

PYLADES: Yes.
Or able to make a case on its own merits.
If you won't argue for yourself, you know,
at the very least you can save Electra.
You can make the point that you acted entirely alone.
Am I right?

ORESTES: Right.

PYLADES: Is that right?

ORESTES: Yes.
And not just wait here for their word,
not die cringing,
without speaking a word in my defense.

[*Calculating*]

You're right.

[*Looking at Electra*]

Should we bring Electra with us?

PYLADES: No. Leave her here.
You don't want her volunteering to share the blame.
The court is gathering now.
There's no more time for talk.

ORESTES: Why are you doing this, Pylades,
staying with me now?

PYLADES: I'm your friend, Orestes. People know we do things together. Times like these are the test of whether a person has any capacity for friendship, love, loyalty. If I pass this test I won't care what other judgment anyone makes of me. I'm here to take care of you.

ORESTES: But my mind—you know,
the way that it goes off—
if I were to start all at once to:
go off the subject.

PYLADES: I'll be with you.

ORESTES: Thank you, Pylades.
We've become good friends, you and I.

NURSE 1: In just a moment.

[*The* NURSES *grab Orestes before he can exit. They stand him in a white porcelain tub, strip him of his hospital gown and ritually give him a sponge bath. They dress him in a light gray agnes b. conservative suit. They comb his hair and spray it lightly. A dreamlike atmosphere.* ELECTRA *continues to sing.*]

ORESTES: Well, we talked. We had a few kisses. She was in the pantry with me, and we went down the stairs to the beach. I said: do you want to go for a swim, but she said no, so I took off my clothes and went into the water. I thought, well: she'll wait for me, but then when I came up again she was running, so I grabbed her by the ankle, that's when she fell, if she hurt her back I don't know.

Well, she was in the pantry, you could call it the kitchen, or the mud room. I went in and found her there, and we went into the dining room together that's where we had some kisses. And I said, you want to swim? And she said, in the pool? No, I said, in the ocean. But she started running toward the pool,

I thought it was a game, so I ran after her and caught her by the thigh, you know, or foot, whatever, she came down hard, I don't know what happened then, I don't remember.

I might have caught her rib-cage in my hand. You know, I might have grabbed her there. I, you know, we knew each other, I'd seen her around. You know, as far as that goes, I mean we had been kissing in the pantry, or in the dining room, I think she liked that all right. But then she was shaking, I guess she'd had a chill, I don't know, she might have hurt herself when she fell, because I don't think I did that to her, I don't remember. I might have, you know, held her down a little bit.

TAPEMOUTH MAN [*Speaking elegiacally.*]: In tort law, rulings about product liability first began with objects that entered the human body, such as food and drink, or were directly applied to the body's surface, such as cosmetics, soap, before being extended to objects in less immediate relation to the body—as, for example, the container for food.

And the most obvious, continuous manifestation of the degree to which body and state are interwoven is the fact that one's citizenship ordinarily contains physical presence within the boundaries of that country.

It is because political learning is deeply embodied that the alteration of the political configuration of a country, continent, or hemisphere so often appears to require the alteration of human bodies through war.

While in peacetime a person may absorb the political reality into his body by lifting his eyebrows in a certain manner, by employing a particular kind of handshake or salutation, in war his agreement is registered by entering a certain terrain and participating in certain acts—and consenting to the tearing out of his forehead, eyebrows, and eyes. The arms and legs that are, in peacetime, lent out to the state for a few seconds and then reclaimed may in war be permanently loaned in injured and lost limbs.

There is a literalness about this, about the way the nation inscribes itself in the body, the literalness with which the human body opens itself and allows the nation to be registered in the wound.

And what is remembered in the body is well remembered, and quietly displayed across the surviving generations. The record of the war survives in the bodies, both alive and buried, of the people who were hurt there—just as, from day to day, the nation is embodied in the gestures and the postures, the customs and behavior of its citizens.

[*A* NURSE *replaces the tape over his mouth.*]

[*Here begins The Trial.*]

WILLIAM: The trial will come to order then.

[*The participants in the trial all enter at once.*]

The trial will come to order.
Is there a speaker?

[*During the trial, there are two levels of text: one delivered in the foreground, one in the background, sometimes simultaneously. The foreground text, which is mostly what we hear, is all about private—indeed, intimate—life. The background text, which we mostly don't hear, is the text of public life, the trial— which is treated as so irrelevant that even those speaking it sometimes neglect to listen to it. In short, the judicial system is in ruins. This is the Crazy Trial. First, here is the foreground text: the nurses are speaking. They sit at a table, where there is a microphone, as though they were on a radio talkshow, and we hear their voices over loudspeakers.*]

NURSE 2: This friend of mine met her husband through a newspaper ad?

NURSE 1: Right.

NURSE 2: And so now he's beating her up,

NURSE 1: What did she expect?

NURSE 2: and threatening he'll commit suicide if she leaves.

NURSE 1: She should leave.

NURSE 3: Who was that put herself in a bag full of shit?

NURSE 1: I don't remember.

NURSE 3: Of course you do. Because of her stepfather.

NURSE 2: Right.
These people,
you know,
where I come from they still arrange marriages.

NURSE 1: Can you believe it?

NURSE 2: I wouldn't mind it.

NURSE 3: You say so.

NURSE 2: I wouldn't.

NURSE 3: They say you marry for love, and then it's nothing but trouble.

NURSE 1: It would be nice to have it settled.

NURSE 2: And just live with it.

NURSE 1: Have your family looking out for you.

NURSE 2: Oh, sure.
[*Sarcastically*]
Then you could just relax and live your life.

[*They all laugh.*]

For me, I'm turned down 70 percent of the time I want sex now. It's been five years since I had as much sex as I want and I keep trying to adjust to less sex. Doing porno films really helps satisfy my appetite.

Right after I left my husband and was getting less sex than I wanted, I used to masturbate for 5 minutes in the morning when I woke up. Soon, I was doing it for 2 hours.

Same thing at night, soon masturbating for 4 hours before going to sleep.

I'm not saying this to brag, and I'm not making it up.

I had constantly repeating orgasms, one after the other. I was a slave to my orgasms. It took six hours a day out of my life that I could have been doing other things. One time, I was playing with myself so much it was interfering with a job I had. My boyfriend pulled the vibrator cord out of the wall and said, "You gotta get out of bed." I felt ashamed I was so attached to my body I would do something so awful. I never had that urge to masturbate when I was living with my husband, who was fucking me all the time.

So when I started doing films, that urge started to curb after six months. Now I hardly ever masturbate more than an hour. Usually I'm very happy with a half hour. I try to explain to my boyfriends that, for me, masturbation is not the same as cock sex. And oral sex is not the same as vaginal-cock sex or masturbation.

It's like the difference between beef and ham.

I get a different satisfaction from holding a person I love next to me than holding a person who is just an acquaintance. Different dildos and vibrators feel different. So I get a different feeling when I have a vibrator up my vagina and somebody's fucking me in the ass, or if I have a vibrator in my ass and somebody's manipulating my clitoris with his finger. Even the orgasms are different for me.

Once I've masturbated I may stop at that, or I may feel like having something else next. I may want to go on to another thing. Or I may want to do only one thing for six months.

[*The following dialogue—though it, too, is foreground text—overlaps the preceding solo, so that not much of it is heard.*]

NOD: I'm not one of these guys who thinks you ought to hunt somebody down. But, you hear what some of these guys say who are coming back now . . .

JOHN: about what they saw on the ground—

NOD: the atrocities, the horror stories you hear, I forget,

JOHN: and about one of our guys who was captured and dragged through the streets, and you've got to believe the people who actually perpetrated these tortures are going to be held accountable.

NOD: How are you going to find these people?

JOHN: They'll be found.

NOD: How are you going to find them?

JOHN: They have ways of—you know,

NOD: their neighbors know who they are.

JOHN: Right, and people who protect them who will probably just get a little tired of protecting them.

NOD: I think we're going to get satisfaction on the whole war crime aspect.

[*And this dialogue from the trial is spoken further in the background, underneath the foreground text, and is not heard at all.*]

MENELAUS: I must say, speaking as a man of Agamemnon's generation—there was a man of character I may say: in contrast, for whatever reason, to this younger generation, which strikes one as being made of cheap, malicious stuff. And I ask myself: shall parents never be safe in their own homes? Shall children be the judges, juries, and executioners of their parents?

JOHN [*With indifference*]: They should be stoned to death.

MENELAUS: Both Orestes and Electra should be punished. But banished. Not killed.

NOD: I think they should be stoned to death. Their throats slit. Their eyes gouged out. Their gold teeth pulled. Their flesh should be boiled off their skulls to make table ornaments for sweethearts. And their bones should be carved into letter openers.

I'd like to read something into the record.

WILLIAM: Go ahead.

NOD [*Reading*]: Manny waited until they were finished. "Now," he said, "I know you fellows are unhappy because your girlfriends are sleeping with the Arabs and you've had to sell your Volkswagens to meet next month's mortgage payment, but I'm here to make you laugh in spite of yourselves. . . ."

"Go ahead and do it then, you kosher cocksucker!" yelled the big drunk.

"I wish to thank you for telling it like it is," Manny said very quietly. "Now, if you'll stop finger-fucking your lady under the tablecloth I'll get on with my act."

[*Silence among the foreground actors. The action stops. The following text is heard alone. Then the foreground speakers resume, drowning this out.*]

"You better. It's almost sunrise."

"OK, then, have you heard the one about the chocolate soldier who went to bed with the chocolate mail-order girl?"

"Yes!"

"All right, then, have you heard the one about the President and Nancy's big surprise for him?"

"You told that one last night."

"You were here last night."

"Yes!"

"Well, fucker, that makes two of us who are stupid. The only difference is that I'm getting paid!"

JOHN [*Speaking inaudibly*]: ——

NOD [*Almost inaudibly*]: I didn't.

JOHN: Somebody did.

NOD: I didn't do it.

JOHN: Well, somebody put pubic hair on my Coke can.

NOD: So, somebody put pubic hair on my Coke can, too.

JOHN: I'm saying, somebody put pubic hair on *my* Coke can.

NOD: I'm saying, somebody put pubic hair on my Coke can, too.

JOHN: Are you saying I put pubic hair on your Coke can?

NOD [*Backing off*]: I'm not saying anything.

JOHN: Is that what you're saying?

NOD [*Walking away*]: I'm not saying anything.

[*The Coke can conversation occurs under the following speeches.*]

NURSE 1: I like it gentle, gentle as a lamb. That's why I like faggots a lot. Once you break a faggot they're one of the best lovers you can find.

NURSE 2: Break a faggot? How do you do that?

NURSE 1: You get into their trip and you understand them . . . while you're lusting over them, then you take too many downers with them . . . or rather you make them take too many downers. . . .

NURSE 2: You mean while they're lying there helpless you just do your evil heterosexual thing with them?

NURSE 1: No, well, they have to move, that's the whole trip. When I was a lot younger my girlfriend and I would hitch over to the Gold Cup Restaurant, dressed up in male costumes. I had short hair then and we'd trap some young gay guy and we'd take him home and just flip him out. He'd scream. One was totally terrified when he found out we were really women.

But it's worth it, you know, because they're so sensual, and, of course, it's an ego trip, I mean, you know, a control trip.

[*And, in the background*]

PYLADES: Orestes deserves a crown! What he did was avenge his father's murder by killing a worthless whore. A woman, moreover, who kept men back
from waging war, kept them at home, tormented by the fear that, if they left,
those who stayed behind would seduce their wives and destroy their families
and homes.

TYNDAREUS: It's a nightmare really.

NOD: And why should Clytemnestra not take a lover? All the wives did when
their husbands were at war. These men were gone for *years*, whoring their
way through the east, while Clytemnestra stayed at home.

[*The following is a fragment of the archaic Greek world.*]

ORESTES: Men of Argos, it was for your sake as much as for my father that I
killed my mother.

If you sanction the murder of husbands by wives, you might as well go kill
yourselves right now or accept the domination of your women.

If you vote that I must die,
then you are all as good as dead,
since wives will have the courage of their crimes.

NOD: A good argument, but not good enough, in fact, a sort of cheap, brag-
ging blabber when you come down to it. Man talk. I mean: Would the same
argument apply if he had killed his father? These men think they can get away
with murder.

JOHN: How's that?

NOD: Let's say he killed his father because his father had killed his mother.

JOHN: Right.

NOD: I mean, would there be any doubt? There's only a doubt because the
person he killed was a woman.

JOHN: Good point.

NOD: So I say he ought to be stoned. And Electra with him, as an accessory to the crime.

ORESTES: I'd like to call an expert witness.

WILLIAM: Go right ahead.

[*Foreground and background come together now.*]

ORESTES: This is Dr. Tabitha Whitlock.

NURSE 1 [*Reading from Dr. Whitlock's testimony*]: I'd just like to say that in a case hinging on the question of parentage, jurisprudence will take into account the possibility of in vitro fertilization.

[*General uproar*]

NOD: Are you saying that Orestes is the product of in vitro fertilization?

NURSE 1: It may not be necessary to establish that he is, in order to establish certain apposite legal principles. Indeed, there is precedent in the common law, in any case, for regarding the mother only as the nurse of the seed implanted by the father—so that the father is the parent, sine qua non, and the mother merely the incubator. For without the father, there is no child; the father is the uncaused cause.

Then, too, on the question of parenting altogether, leaving aside the question of parentage, it was Clytemnestra herself who compromised or voided the sanctity of the mother-child relationship years before the event for which Orestes and Electra are now on trial—or certainly voided it by the murder of their children's own father.

NOD: This is an argument more clever than true.
The young man is guilty.
His sister's guilty, too.

TYNDAREUS: We're all agreed to that.

[*The following is another fragment of the archaic Greek world.*]

ORESTES: Men of Argos, we accept your verdict, having no other choice.
But let it not be death by stoning.
Rather let us take our own lives,
and in that way we ourselves
will end the chain of murder
that has cursed the House of Atreus,
and with our deaths let us restore
the public order.

NOD: We accept your decision if there is no quarrel.

[*Beat*]

Silence is assent.
The trial is ended.

[*Silence.* ORESTES *pisses in his pants, and urine slowly runs over the stage. We hear a huge soprano aria from Berlioz'* Les Troyens. *As Orestes continues to piss, the others all leave. Lights darken to twilight.*]

TAPEMOUTH MAN [*Cheerfully, like a smiling Buddha*]:
The imagination
is less a separate faculty
than a quality of all our mental faculties:
the quality of seeing more things
and making more connections among ideas about things
than any list of theories and discourses
can countenance.
The imagination works
by a principle of sympathy
with the suppressed and subversive elements in experience.
It sees the residues,
the memories, and the reports of past or faraway social worlds
and of neglected or obscure perceptions
as the main stuff with which we remake our contexts.
It explains the operation of a social order
by representing what the remaking of this order would require.
It generalizes our ideas
by tracing a penumbra of remembered or intimated possibility

around present or past settlements.
By all these means
it undermines
the identification of the actual
with the possible.

[NOD, JOHN, *and* WILLIAM *put the tape back over the man's mouth, pick him up, carry him, in his wheelchair, upstage, put him down sideways on the ground facing away from the audience; when John and William turn away to go back to their places, Nod kicks the Tapemouth Man in the head three times, or shoots him in the head.*]

ELECTRA: Orestes,
I don't think I can bear it.
To die.
To be gone forever.

ORESTES: Electra.

[*From here on, the piece takes on a slurred, dizzying speed.*]

ELECTRA: If only I could give my life in place of yours,
Orestes.
It makes me dizzy.
It makes me feel a little light . . .
Not to see you ever again.
To be gone.
Not to be with you, or anyone,
or anywhere.
Not to see anything, or touch it,
not to know it's there.

To be here,
to see you,
to see the world around me,
to feel my body,
and to think then,
all of a sudden,
it will be gone.

I like almost anything that falls from the sky—
you know, snow, hail—
sleet even, when the sleet is mingled with very white snow.
Or anything that's white.
Or duck eggs.

Or things that always give you a clean feeling, like
a new metal bowl,
or an earthen pottery cup,
or a new wooden chest.

Or things that give you an unclean feeling.
The inside of a cat's ear.
A rat's nest.

I've gotten involved with a lot of men I didn't like,
as odd as that seems,
so lately
I didn't know what to do with someone I did like.

And I never have come with a man,
always before or after,
and it gets more and more difficult
as time goes on.
Maybe it's just
the way I'm made.

On New Year's Eve one time,
I knew a man who kissed me two times—
kisses so sweet,
so remote,
so much of something from a different time.

I tell myself:
Well, our time has come.
This happens.
I've thought about it all my life;
it always used to seem
completely normal.

But now, you think:
it's inconceivable.

You think: when you die, you never come back.
And you don't know where you are.

ORESTES: I don't think about it.
We have one choice left, that's all,
to choose the way we have to die.

ELECTRA: I can't do that.

ORESTES: When it comes to it, we all have a preference.
Some people cut their wrists . . .
Some people tie their hands with wire . . .

[*Silence*]

ELECTRA: Then, I want you to kill me.

ORESTES: What?

ELECTRA: I want you to kill me.

ORESTES [*To himself*]: God . . .

ELECTRA: I can't do it myself,
I can't let some stranger do it.

ORESTES: My hands are still covered with my mother's blood.
I can't do it, Electra.
We'll each have to—
take our own lives.

[*Silence*]

ELECTRA: Then promise me:
Let me die first.

ORESTES: I promise.

ELECTRA: And let me hold you.

[*They embrace.*]

I love you, Orestes.

[*Beat*]

I wish we could share one grave.

[*Music. They dance. We hear the following text, in Electra's voice, over the music.*]

All I ever had in mind was to do the right thing. I got one or two things at auction, thinking they might be all right, a chair, and a few little paintings, nothing special. I hadn't even thought it might be a Constable, I only thought that it was pretty, and this man Keating came to dinner and absolutely berated me for it. "I can tell you," he said, "beyond the shadow of a doubt that this painting has nothing to do with John Constable." "Well," I said . . . "Nothing whatever," he said. "If it were a Constable, it would be worth five or six million plus. But no, it's not a Constable. It's not even an F. W. Watts. It's not even a John Paul! Well, maybe it's a Paul."

I hadn't even cared until he said all that to me, but then I began to cry, thinking I can do nothing right, not even when I'm not trying. I must be just incorrectly positioned, I think I always was, from the start, the way it is when you can never get the right grip on anything because you're at the wrong end, or on the wrong side of it! And I wanted everything to be just fragile.

[PYLADES *enters.*]

PYLADES: Orestes.

What's happening?

ORESTES: We've been condemned to death, Pylades.
It's over.

[*This scene is on speed.*]

PYLADES: You're giving up?

ORESTES: It's finished.
You'll be the next to go on trial.

[*Silence*]

PYLADES: Well, if what you say is true
—and there's no hope for us—
OK.
Then:
Let's take Menelaus with us.

ORESTES: What?

PYLADES: These good men think this game is all played out,
but there are some moves still to be made.

ORESTES: Try to see it as it is: this is the end.

PYLADES: Not at all.
The end is when you're dead,
your insides are torn out
and your bones are scattered whitened on the ground.
You mean to say you'll just stand by and watch your sister die?
Menelaus could have saved her at least.
Could have spoken up.
Could have pleaded for her life.
Could have argued leniency for her at least.
The hero of Troy—
could have spent some little credit on behalf of your sister,
instead of hoarding it all for himself and for his wife Helen.
But—tell me, Orestes—
you wouldn't want to hurt him?

ORESTES: I'd hurt Menelaus if there were any way.

PYLADES: The way is there.
We only have to take it.

ORESTES: What way?

PYLADES: Cut Helen's throat.

ORESTES: Cut Helen's throat.

PYLADES: Right.

ORESTES: Now I feel dizzy.

[*He sits.*]

ELECTRA: Cut Helen's throat . . .

PYLADES: The act itself would give me pleasure,
and whose fault is all this if it isn't Helen's fault?

ORESTES: You blame it all on her?

PYLADES: No one would disagree with that.
Who do you think they all gossip about?

ORESTES: They gossip about everything.

ELECTRA: Cut Helen's throat . . .

[*Silence.*]

ORESTES: What sort of scheme is this?

PYLADES: If justice is what's wanted,
let's have justice.

ORESTES: This isn't justice.

PYLADES: This is a just revenge.

ORESTES: Yes, you mean:
if we're going to die,
let's bring them all down with us.

PYLADES: But then:
Why speak of dying?

ORESTES [*Shouting*]: We are going to die, Pylades.
Is nothing clear to you in your mind?
We're going to die!

PYLADES [*Shouting*]: Not necessarily.

[*Quietly*]

Think it through.
Let's say, after we kill her,
we kidnap her daughter.

ELECTRA [*Musing*]: Hermione.

PYLADES: Lure her to us, hold her as a hostage.

ELECTRA [*Coming alert*]: Use her for safe passage out of town.

PYLADES: For all three of us.

ELECTRA: This is the way to save your life, Orestes.

ORESTES: To save my life. . . .

PYLADES: This is the way to save your sister's life.
It comes to this:
you have a choice now between your sister's life and Helen's.
Which one will you sacrifice to save the other?

ELECTRA: I can't believe it's right,
finally,
after all this, for you to sacrifice your life to save Helen.

ORESTES: This is my choice?

PYLADES: You do something in the world. You take an action.
That's a commitment.

You have to see it through, you know?
You bring other people along with you,
you have an obligation.
Some people think you can go through life saying.
oh, I take it back,
no, I apologize,
that isn't what I meant at all.
Let's start all over again.
Some people think: well, I can always take it back.
But that's not the case.
Some things, it happens just like that—

[*Snaps his fingers.*]
And that's a done deal.
That's where you are in your life.

[*Silence as he lets this sink in, then:*]

It's going to be all right. You'll see how fast Menelaus meets our demands,
when he sees his wife in a pool of blood and a knife at his daughter's throat.
And everyone who sees this will know that finally justice has been done.

ELECTRA: This is so clear.

ORESTES: We start this all over again?

[*Beat*]

ELECTRA: This is the right thing, Orestes.
This feels right to me.

[*Long silence. Slow motion.*]

PYLADES: I've tried to think of this as you would yourself.
The kind of person you are—
those qualities that first drew me to you to be your friend.
I've tried to put myself in your place.
And this is right for you.

ELECTRA: Listen to him, Orestes.
this is a person who knows the world and how it works.
This is a person you can count on.

ORESTES: I don't feel well.
We've come full circle.
We'll take some time to think this through.

PYLADES: There's no time.

ORESTES: I don't know.
I'm not thinking clearly now.
We need some time.

PYLADES: There wasn't time after you made your first move!
This is it.
Make your next move.

ELECTRA: Let's do it.
Let's do this.

PYLADES [*Quietly*]: What kind of man would throw away his sister's life?

[*Silence*]

ORESTES [*Quietly*]: I'll go along with it.

[*They all exit. It is very quiet. Silence. The men are in bed.*]

WILLIAM: Do you think forgiveness is possible?

JOHN: Uh, primarily, uh, uh, the, uh, the . . . primarily the question is does man have the power to forgive himself. And he does. That's essentially it. I mean if you forgive yourself, and you absolve yourself of all, uh, of all wrongdoing in an incident, then you're forgiven. Who cares what other people think, because uh . . .

WILLIAM: Was this a process you had to go through over a period of time. Did you have to think about it?

JOHN: Well, no. Not until I was reading the Aquarian gospel did I, did I strike upon, you know I had almost had ends meet because I had certain uh you know to-be-or-not-to-be reflections about of course what I did. And uh,

WILLIAM: I'm sorry, what was that?

JOHN: Triple murder. Sister, husband. Sister, husband, and a nephew, my nephew. And uh, you know, uh, manic depressive.

WILLIAM: Do you mind my asking what instruments did you use? What were the instruments?

JOHN: It was a knife. It was a knife.

WILLIAM: Knife?

JOHN: Yes.

WILLIAM: So then, the three of them were all . . .

JOHN: Sssssss . . .
[*Points to slitting his throat*]
like that.

WILLIAM: So, uh, do you think that as time goes by, this episode will just become part of your past, or has it already . . .

JOHN: It has already become part of my past.

WILLIAM: Has already become part of your past. No sleepless nights? No . . .

JOHN: Aw, no. In the first three or four years there was a couple of nights where I would stay up thinking about how I did it, you know. And what they said . . . they told me later there were so many stab wounds in my sister and I said no, that's not true at all, you know. So I think I had a little blackout during the murders, but uh . . .

WILLIAM: I'm sorry, they said there were many stab wounds . . .

JOHN: Well, uh, they said there was something like thirty stab wounds in my sister, and I remember distinctly I just cut her throat once. That was all, you know, and I don't know where the thirty stab wounds came from. So that might have been some kind of blackout thing. You know, I was trying to re- re- re- uh, re- uh, uh, resurrect the uh, the crime—my initial steps, etc. You know, and uh, and uh, I took, as a matter of fact, it came right out of the, I was starting the New Testament at the time, matter of fact I'm about the only person you'll ever meet that went to, to do a triple murder with a Bible in his, in his pocket, and, and, listening to a radio. I had delusions of grandeur with the radio. Uh, I had a red shirt on that was symbolic of, of some lines in Revelation, in the, in the New Testament. Uh I had a red motor . . . as a matter of fact, I think it was chapter 6 something, verses 3, 4, or 5, or something where uh it was a man, it was a man. On a red horse. And, and, a man on a red horse came out, and uh, and uh uh, and he was given a knife, and unto him was given the power to kill and destroy. And I actually thought I was this person. And I thought that my red horse was this red Harley Davidson I had. And I wore . . . it was just, you know, it was kind of a symbolic type of thing. And and and uh, you know, uh after the murders I thought the nephew was, was the, was a new devil or something, you know. This, this is pretty bizarre now that I think back on it. I thought he was a new devil and uh, uh. I mean basically I love my sister, there's no question about that. But at times my sister hadn't come through uh for me. You know and I was in another, one of these manic attacks. And uh, and uh, uh, uh, you know, uh, I was just uh, I was just you know, I mean I was fed up with all this you know one day they treat me good and then they tell all these other people that I was a maniac and watch out for me and etc. and like that. And uh, uh, so I went to them that night to tell them I was all in trouble again, you know, and could they put me up for the night, you know, and they told me to take a hike and uh so uh, believing that I had the power to kill, uh you know, that was that for them. You know. I mean when family turns you out, that's a real blow. You know. But uh, back to the original subject of forgiveness. If I forgive myself I'm forgiven. You know that's essentially the answer. I'm the captain of my own ship. I run my own ship. Nobody can crawl in my ship unless they get permission. I just [*He nods.*] "over there." You know. "I'm forgiven." You know. Ha-ha. You know. [*Laughs.*] It's as simple as that. You know. You're your own priest, you're your own leader, you're your own captain. You know. You run your own show, a lot of people know that.

NOD: What do you think of the soaps?

JOHN: What?

NOD: The soaps.

JOHN: You mean the daytimes?

NOD: Right.

JOHN: They're OK.

NOD: I think they're wonderful. I think the clothes could be better, and they could use some comic relief, you know, but otherwise I think they're wonderful. Although, of course, I guess they could use some more fantasy. You know. In times like these, we need a little more "I wanna be," and not so much "I am."

JOHN: Unh-hunh.

NOD: I think it's incredible how much excellence you see in the scenes.

JOHN: Unh-hunh.

NOD: Although I think they could have more minority representation. And I think they should move faster. You know, they should have shorter stories— beginning, middle, end, like that, and not just have the same story go on for a year or something. I mean they get lost in the past, they don't quite catch up with the times. You know, I like to see some stuff going on, I don't just want to watch my next door neighbors.

Do you think they're too believable?

JOHN: No.

WILLIAM: Yes, I do. That's what I would say.

NOD: I'm a little tired of seeing spouses coming back from the dead all the time and plots with missing babies. I think that's a little too obvious.

JOHN: To me, my only complaint would be that most shows are overly lit.

NOD: Too bright.

JOHN: Exactly.

[*Horrible cries from offstage. The* PHRYGIAN *enters at a dead run shouting, first to the men in bed, and then, as they enter, to the nurses.*]

PHRYGIAN [*Speaking at breakneck speed*]:
Oh God, God
Trojans, women, children, slaves—
terror screaming
fall upon you from the sky
cut your knees
cut women come home

NOD: Who's this?

WILLIAM: This is Helen's servant.

NOD: Oh.

PHRYGIAN: Oh,
hill of Tigris,
sacred city,
poets, learned men,
temples, courtyards,
little, little fountains
children play
for pride
more than rubble
stone from stone
courtyards,
bedrooms opened to the sky
graves and craters
all for Helen.

[*The* NURSES *grab him and hustle him to bed; he continues, taking his time to speak distinctly.*]

These are men, mind you.
They threw their arms around the lady's knees,
begging for their lives.

And then, suddenly,
they attack.
Suddenly there is terror.
Suddenly confusion.
Suddenly the servants scatter
in all directions, crying out:

[*Resuming breakneck speed*]

"Lookout, lady!"
Too late, too late.
"Lookout, lady!"
as they run.
"Lookout, lady!"
Rush away, falling, stumbling stairs
cry out: Treachery!
Treachery!

And it is done.

[*The* NURSES *give him an injection.*]

NURSE 3: It's OK now.
Tell me quietly.
Where were you.

PHRYGIAN: Next to her, fanning her
a round feather fan
gentle breeze

[*Smoke has begun to fill the stage. He is beginning to go to sleep.*]

her hand reached up
her fingers wound themselves around the fan
caught up in feathers
let her yarn fall to the floor

And Orestes shouting to the slaves to go
They fell on her like wild boars

like wild boars come snuffling through the woods
and screaming
Die!

[*Spent*]

The lady screamed,
snow white arms reaching out.
Her fingers caught in her own hair
tearing out her hair
collapsing to the floor.

[*He is close to sleep now.*]

But then, just as she sank to the ground,
Hermione came in

[*More smoke*]

the men stopped—
as for an instant
from respect
and shame.

But
then they turned and seized the girl
their new victim.

When suddenly
Helen vanished.

[*He's very sleepy now, partly dreaming.*]

Vanished.
They turned around
she was gone.
As though she
passed right through the roof.
And she was gone.

As though
stolen by the gods.

The cause of war—
has been removed—
is gone—
and all that's left—
is
ruin.

[*He is asleep.*]

NOD: There was a guy checked in here once—were you on the floor then?—
who had this old shoebox full of female genitalia. Did you see that? He had
nine vulvas. This is a true story. Most were dried and shriveled, though one
had been sort of daubed with silver paint and trimmed with a red ribbon.
Another one, the one on top, seemed really fresh. He had part of the mons
veneris with the vagina and anus attached. And when you looked real close
you could see little crystals on it, he had sprinkled it with crystals of salt.

Another box, he had four noses, human noses, and there was a Quaker Oats
box with scraps of human head integument.

And several pairs of leggings he had made, and a vest that he had made from
the torso of a woman, tanned like leather, with a string on it so you could pull
it up and wear it, breasts and all.

And masks that he had made by peeling the faces from the skulls of different
women. Of course they had no eyes, just holes where the eyes had been. But
the hair was still attached to the scalps. A few were all dried out, but some of
them had been treated with oil, to keep the skin smooth and lifelike, and
some had lipstick on their lips. If you had known them, and you had seen
their masks, you would have recognized them.

[MENELAUS *rushes in—in a panic—his* BODYGUARD *behind him.*]

MENELAUS: What's happened here?
Where is my wife?

[*The palace is in flames. Smoke fills the stage. Dimly visible through the smoke,* ORESTES *and* PYLADES *appear on the roof of the palace. They have Hermione between them. Orestes holds a knife at her throat. Further back* ELECTRA *stands, holding a torch.*]

MENELAUS: Who let this happen?
Is that my daughter?

[*Instantly out of control*]

What the fuck is this, Orestes, you fucking madman.
Who let him up there?
Get your fucking hands off her, Orestes.
How did they get up there?
Get him the fuck down here.
What the fuck do you think you're doing?

ORESTES: Do you want to ask your questions, Menelaus, or do you want me to give you some answers first?

MENELAUS: What the fuck sort of question is that?

ORESTES: In case it is of any interest to you, I am going to kill your daughter.

MENELAUS: I am going to have your fucking ass, Orestes.
You are dead meat, you fucking nut case,
Who the fuck let him up there?
You won't walk away from this alive.

ORESTES: No, I'm not walking anywhere, until I've burned this fucking house down, and you've brought in a helicopter to fly us out.
Otherwise, your daughter is dead meat.

MENELAUS: What have you done with Helen?

ORESTES: I don't remember.

MENELAUS: Don't fuck with me!

ORESTES: I think she's gone.

MENELAUS: Gone where?

ORESTES: I think she's gone to heaven.

MENELAUS: Don't fuck with me, Orestes.

ORESTES [*Very offhanded, chilling*]: Really, I think she's gone to heaven.
I meant to kill her. I really did.
But then the gods came down and spirited her away.
Something like that.

MENELAUS: Where is she?

ORESTES: You don't believe me?
You don't think the gods would do that for her?
I can't help what you think, Menelaus.
She's disappeared.

MENELAUS: You surrender her body to me for burial, or I'll fuck you up.

ORESTES [*Screams.*]: I didn't kill her.

[*Controlled*]

Now your daughter: that's another matter.
I'm going to cut her throat right before your eyes unless you arrange to get us
out of here.

[*Fire is now everywhere.*]

MENELAUS [*Turning to the others onstage, in a quiet but urgent tone of
voice*]: Can't you get someone up there?

ORESTES: What is your answer, Menelaus?

MENELAUS: Haven't you had enough of killing?

ORESTES: I never get enough of killing whores!

MENELAUS: I'll have his fucking ass!

[*Sounds of a helicopter. Police and fire lights. Loudspeaker voice with instructions to "Stand back." "Stand back from the car." "Get back there!" etc.*]

MENELAUS: Go ahead and kill her, then, you fuck.
I'm giving you nothing!
You think you can jerk me around!

ORESTES: OK, I will!

MENELAUS: No, no, for God's sake.
[*Uncontrolled weeping and wailing and crying out*]
Oh, God, he's got my daughter up there.
[*Collapsing to his knees weeping*]
This fucking madman has my daughter.

[*The voice of Apollo over a loudspeaker.*]

APOLLO: All right.
That's enough.
Everyone stay calm.
This is Apollo speaking.
Put down your knife, Orestes.
And listen, all of you,

[APOLLO *enters, accompanied by bodyguards. He wears a conservative gray suit. With him is Helen, now in the form of a giant blow-up fuck-me doll. Apollo's voice continues to be miked so that he can speak very quietly, in the manner and accent of whoever is the current American president, and his voice still fills the theater.*]

to what I have to say.
Let's hope things have not gone so far
that not even a god can put them to right!

[*He smiles at his own little tension-relieving joke.*]

You see, with me, I have Helen.
Orestes, as you can see, did her no harm.
I rescued her, at the command of Zeus, her father.

Understand:
because Zeus is her father, Helen could not die—
although she has gone to heaven,
having caused enough anguish here below.
She will take her place there in the sky,
like a beautiful, bright star,
a guide to mariners forevermore.
Such is Helen's end.
You see how things work out
when you approach things with a little patience and goodwill,
some thought to the long-term good of all,
a sense of charity,
respect,
a due regard for the good opinion of mankind.

Indeed, what you see written in the stars can as well be rewritten with a sense
of what is right, with a sense of warmth and compassion.

That's why I say to all of you here:
watch
and learn.

[*The city goes on burning, even as Apollo speaks. And, one by one, those who
listen to him become bored and stop listening. The nurses are the first, returning
to their game of mah jong.*]

Orestes, for example: henceforth, it is ordained that he will take a long trip.
And when he returns to the city of Athens, he will be ensured a fair and im-
partial trial. I myself will preside. And see to it that he is not unduly punished.

[*Looking around, hands outstretched*]

Let us not forget, after all, who he is, and the family that he comes from.

[NOD *turns on the radio, and now we hear music under Apollo's voice.*]

In time to come, Orestes will marry Hermione.
And the two of them will live in great joy together.

As for Electra, a life of wedded happiness awaits her, too,
with her husband Pylades.

[*One by one, all but Apollo take seats, or lie down or wander out.*]

And Menelaus will leave the rule of Argos to Orestes. Menelaus himself will
reign in Sparta—the rightful dowry of his beloved wife Helen.

This is a land whose citizens have always believed,
and still believe today, that they have a heritage,
they have a civilization and a culture,
a set of practices and well-known customs
values and ideals
that are the rightful envy of the world.
This is what I believe.
The traditions that help them make a world that will endure
as long as their faith and their goodwill remain intact
and they share their gifts with all those in the world born less fortunate than
     they.
Then may we say with confidence truly this is a blessed people, the rightful
     envy of the world.

[*Apollo is left alone at center stage. His* BODYGUARDS *step forward and pick him
up unceremoniously, like a piece of furniture, and carry him out. The city
remains a smoking ruin, a smoldering fire. The quiet of a hospital ward. The
music on Nod's radio continues—like the music that continues on the radio after
a car wreck.* NURSE 3 *enters and goes to one of the beds.*]

NURSE 3: Are you William?

JOHN: Over there.

NURSE 3: I've come to change your dressing.

WILLIAM: Oh, yes.

NURSE 3: I guess you'll be dressing for dinner, eh?

WILLIAM: Yes.

NURSE 3: Do you have any pain?

WILLIAM: Oh, yes.
I'd say that's the least of it.
I'd say:
I'm not myself any more.
My head wrapped in bandages.
More like Lazarus gone into the tomb instead of leaving it.
Listening to the sounds,
someone's foot rapping on the ceiling,
the jailer's keys,
the sound of the water running,
and someone washing their hands
the incessant washing of hands.
I hear city noises from time to time,
they have nothing to do with me any more.
I think:
how beautiful the city used to be in September,
going home after dark.
Our senses ripened in the sun, they used to say,
But now, you'd have to say, people know better how to mind their own
    damned business:
the ability to distinguish between degrees of light,
licking the twilight and floating in the huge open mouth filled with honey
    and shit
horse piss collaborating with the heat of an animal
incubating the baser instincts,
flabby, insipid flesh multiplying itself with the help of computer-assisted gene
    splicing.
We've done a lot of violence to the sniveling tendencies in our natures.
What we need now are some strong, straightforward actions that you'd have
    to be a fool not to learn the wrong lessons from it.

NURSE 3: There, that's all now.

WILLIAM: If you were married to logic,
you'd be living in incest,
swallowing your own tail.

Every man must shout:
there's a great destructive work to be done.
We're doing it!

NURSE 3: That's all now. We're finished.

WILLIAM: Thank you.

[*He sinks back on his pillow, exhausted, and goes to sleep.*]

THE END

The Trojan Women a Love Story

The Trojan Women a Love Story, based on the works of Euripides and Berlioz, was developed with Greg Gunter as dramaturg and incorporates shards of our contemporary world, to lie, as in a bed of ruins, within the frame of the classical world. It uses texts by the survivors of Hiroshima and of the Holocaust, by Slavenka Drakulic, Zlatko Dizdarevic, Georges Bataille, Sei Shonagon, Elaine Scarry, Hannah Arendt, the Kama Sutra, Amy Vanderbilt, and the Geraldo show. It was first staged at the American Repertory Theatre Institute, where it was directed by Robert Woodruff and subsequently directed by Tina Landau at the University of Washington in Seattle. It received its first full production by En Garde Arts in New York, where it was again directed by Tina Landau.

A Note on the Music: There are meant to be many songs in this piece: many romantic, sentimental love songs from the '30s, '40s, '50s, some very twisted songs, some current songs—aggressive, hostile, cutting. I leave it to the director and actors to bring in songs they feel capture the essence of the piece—and so bring their own particular tastes and passions to it.

The Trojan Women a Love Story

Characters

CHORUS OF THIRD WORLD WOMEN,
including

   EISA

   SEI

   AIMABLE

   VALERIE

   CHEA

HECUBA

ANDROMACHE

TALTHYBIUS

BILL

RAY BOB

CASSANDRA

POLYXENA

MENELAUS

HELEN

AENEAS

Casting note: To reduce the number of choral speaking parts, Sei, Aimable, and Valerie can be conflated into a single character.

THE PROLOGUE

Lights out.

Immediately: a deafening wall of sound—from Berlioz' Les Troyens. Sounds under it of gunfire, explosions, screams, fire truck sirens.

Early dawn. As the dawn light comes up very slowly, the Berlioz gradually fades.

The light reveals a hundred dark-skinned "Third World" women making computer components at little work tables. The women are in torn clothes; they are in shock; many have been raped. Some women are lying against a wall, shivering. Or crouching in corners. Their tables are set out on dirt.

Behind them, the city is a smoking, still-burning ruin.

Black ashes rain down continuously on the stage.

As the Berlioz fades from all the speakers, from one speaker the introductory accompaniment for a pop song comes up: and the women—maintaining their expressions and attitudes of being shell-shocked, without affect—sing the Billie Holliday arrangement of "When Somebody Loves You."

At one place onstage there is a body motionless under a blanket. At another place, a pile of rags suddenly moves.

The CHORUS *stops singing abruptly and the women turn to look at the pile of rags.* HECUBA *raises her head from the pile of rags.*

We hear the occasional sound of a howling wind, the pop of a gunshot in the distance.

Hecuba is a grand woman, a diva. She wears a silk Yves Saint Laurent that has been torn. She has been dragged across the city. She is dazed. From time to time, her speaking is interrupted by uncontrollable shivering.

HECUBA: Last night: a child picked up
out of its bed by its feet
taken out to the courtyard
swung round by a soldier in an arc
its head smashed against a tree
all this done while another soldier held back
the child's mother
all this done right before the mother's eyes

and the mother
could not even cry.

I heard a young girl call out
Mama—

[*Hecuba and the other women look suddenly to the side, as though hearing the girl's voice, hold for a moment before Hecuba resumes.*]

the last word she ever spoke.

A child saying to her mother:
Look what I have lived to see before my death.

A world destroyed
by the hands of those who thought
themselves the creators of civilization.

CHORUS MEMBER 1, EISA: This is how men are.

HECUBA: My husband
my sons
all murdered
My home on fire.

The war—
the Greek heroes camped outside our walls
the daily round of murder
the slow, relentless grinding down of our lives
to those of survivors
shuddering suddenly now and then for no reason at all
ten long years—
is ended now;
and yet it goes on without end.
Yesterday, between one streetcar stop and the next
six people were killed, twenty wounded;
two mortar shells
killed five children and wounded twenty;
these are the reports we hear.

They've killed all the young boys
along with the men—
except young Aeneas—
Aeneas, who lies somewhere,
frightened,
hiding in some house or hovel,
some basement,
under some mound of dirt or rubble,
cowering,
saving his own life,
leaving the women to be raped or killed.

Why was this done?

This is beyond knowing.
I pray that I could
pull it all inside my body
all the murder
all the ruin
the fire
the wounds
broken limbs
bleeding childen
my city
bring it all deep inside me
so that I could understand.

CHORUS MEMBER 2, SEI: I had just come into the room and said "good
     morning,"
and suddenly it turned bright red.
I felt hot on my cheeks,
and when I came to,
I realized everyone was lying
on one side of the room.
No one was standing.
The chairs had blown to one side.
There was no window glass.
My white shirt was red all over.
I thought it was funny because
I wasn't hurt.
I looked around
and then I realized
that the girl lying next to me had pieces
of broken glass stuck all over her body.
Her blood had splashed onto my shirt.
And she had bits of wood stuck in her.

SEI: I had been holding my son in my arms,
when a young woman in front of me said, "Please
take this seat."
We were just changing places
when suddenly there was a strange sound.

All at once it was dark
and before I knew it,
I had jumped outside.
Fragments of glass had lodged in my son's head.
But he looked at my face and smiled.
He did not understand what had happened.
I had plenty of milk
which he drank all that day.
I think my child sucked the poison right out of my body.
And soon after that
he died.

HECUBA: Why was this done?

[ANDROMACHE *rushes down front again and picks up a microphone, tries to
speak. She still cannot. Puts down the microphone and retreats upstage.*]

EISA: I was sitting in a box at the opera,
dressed in a new gown.
My hair was done up so beautifully.
And when it came to the line,
"There is the devil,"
a company of enemy soldiers ran in,
stomping their feet,
and came right up to me.
They had a secret machine
that had told them
that when I heard the word devil I thought of their general.
I looked around for help,
but everyone in the audience was staring straight ahead,
not even showing pity for what I'd got myself into.
An elderly gentleman in the box next to mine
looked over at me,
but when I started to speak to him,
he spit in my face.

AIMABLE: I was at a movie,
a very large theater, very dark,
a downtown theater,

and I knew it was wrong for me to be there.
Only enemy soldiers were allowed there.
And their general came in and sat next to me.
And I was more scared than ever.
But he put his arm around me.

[*Tears come to her eyes.*]

And I felt comforted.
He put his hand on me.
Inside my thigh.
And I liked it.

[*She weeps; silence.*]

VALERIE: What should a woman do
when all the men are gone.

EISA: Turned and ran

VALERIE: No, not most of them.
Most kept on
till they were dead.

CHEA: But the smart ones.
They all ran in the end.

AIMABLE: Except Aeneas.

CHEA: Right.
Aeneas.

EISA: Bring him out why don't we?
Sic him on these bastards.

CHEA: Let him be killed, too?
No, let him rest.
Let him recover.
Then let him gather up all the others who ran away

and go after these Greeks the way they came for us—
in the dark like cowards
and pay them back for what they've done to us.

HECUBA: No.
Enough.
Let it end.

There is nothing predestined in all this:
if rage and violence is in our bones
then let us rise beyond it—
this is what it is to be civilized.

Whatever could make you
want to start again?

THE PLAY

[TALTHYBIUS *enters. He wears the standard State Department pin-stripe suit.
He is accompanied by two soldiers from Special Forces,* BILL *and* RAY BOB.]

TALTHYBIUS: Hecuba.
I beg your pardon.
My name is Talthybius.
I come to you
as a liaison from the Greeks.
And with my
—sympathies—
to you and your compatriots.
My regrets I must find you in this . . .
condition.
I am a diplomat,
not a creator of policy.
My charge is to give to policies
set by others
not perhaps what is the best part of myself—
not my heart, or mind, or soul—but
the honest employment of my voice.

BILL: For what is a man
but a tube with two orifices,
anal and buccal.

RAY BOB: This is not you show me yours I'll show you mine.
This is let's bust some balls.
This is how men are.

BILL: I don't say I like it this way.

TALTHYBIUS: And at the same time . . .

RAY BOB: You can accept it.

BILL: I can live with it.

TALTHYBIUS: To be sure
in war
there are no victors.

HECUBA: Are there not?

TALTHYBIUS: I should think not.
Here, at the end
when we would all wish to restore some order,
return to some world of civility,
we discover instead that
the aftermath of war is
a riot in a parrot house.
This is not to my taste, I must say.
I confess I am the sort of man
who enjoys what is familiar.
I have a sweater I like to wear
that I have had since my days at Princeton.
And when I sing
I like to sing the Duke of Plaza Toro
or some other song from Gilbert and Sullivan
or the hymns I learned as a child,
"How Firm a Foundation,"
"The Son of God Goes Forth to War."

I have a favorite walking stick,
I love to tell the stories my father told to me.
I don't think of myself as a rude man
or harsh.
And so I would not say it is in my nature
to have to say to you
that the council of my countrymen
has reached some decisions
about how you women have been allotted
each to a man.

HECUBA: Allotted?

TALTHYBIUS: Yes.

HECUBA: How these women are to be
divided up
among your soldiers?

AIMABLE: As slaves?

TALTHYBIUS: Or wives.

HECUBA: Or wives.

You mean
to do with these women
what they want?

[*Silence*]

And with me, too?

TALTHYBIUS: Yes.

[*Silence*]

HECUBA: And my children.

TALTHYBIUS: Yes.

HECUBA: This is why you come to us
speaking of civility.

Now that the war is over
you can think of nothing better
than to remake the conditions
that are the cause of war.

BILL: The war over?
You say this to the men:
The war is not over, they say,
we are the war,
we ourselves are the war.

RAY BOB: Men act.
We know this.
Attach no value to it,
particularly.
To act is to be.
No more no less.

BILL: A human being can be thought of as a tree trunk on fire.
You can lay them down screaming
on their stomachs or their backs—
or you can spare the fire
and lay them out on the beach
nothing more than breathless lacerations
shapeless silhouettes
half eaten
getting up or moaning on the ground
then you might say
the head—
the eyes, the ears, the brain
represent the complications of the buccal orifice
the penis, the testicles
or you could say
the female organs that correspond to these
are the complications of the anal orifice.
So you have the familiar violent thrusts
that come from the interior of the body

indifferently ejected
from one end of the body or the other
discharged,
that is to say,
wherever they meet the weakest resistance.

RAY BOB: The world is a bleeding wound
when it comes to that.

BILL: The natural state of a man,
the ecstatic state, will find itself in the visions of things that appear suddenly:
    cadavers, for example,
nudity, explosions, spilled blood, sunbursts, abscesses, thunder.

RAY BOB: Everything that exists
destroys itself
when it comes to that.
The sun in the sky,
the stars,
consuming themselves
and dying.
The joy of life that comes into the world
to give itself
and be annihilated.

BILL: I can imagine the earth projected in space
as it is
in reality
like a woman screaming,
her head in flames.

RAY BOB: I remember once
there was this group that had an ape,
tied up with ropes
struggling to break free
but trussed up like a chicken
legs folded back against its body
tied upside down to a stake
planted in the middle of a pit
howling and swallowing dirt

its anus screaming pink and pointing at the sky
like a flower
and all the women around the pit
stripped naked for the work and sweating with pleasure
and anticipation
armed with shovels
filling in the pit with dirt
burying the ape alive
its screams choked on the dirt
until all that remains
is the radiant flower of its anus
touched by pretty white fingers
its violent contractions
helpless as it strangles on the dirt
and all who stand around the pit and watch
are overcome by heat and stupor
their throats choked by sighs
and crying out
eyes moist with tears.

BILL: This is how men are.

TALTHYBIUS: Of course,
nonetheless,
when the rain clears in the evening
and you can see the stars come out over the city
walk to some nice restaurant
where they still retain all the old culinary arts—
no sugar for the after dinner coffee, to be sure,
and the cost of a filet of sole is atrocious—
yet one can believe
a good life is still possible in the world
it may be that there are throat germs everywhere
but one can still attend a concert
or hear a reading of Claudel's poetry.

HECUBA: Tell me:
who shall have my daughter Cassandra?

TALTHYBIUS: She is fortunate.
She is being well taken care of.

HECUBA: Who shall have her?

TALTHYBIUS: King Agamemnon.

[*Orchestral music is heard.*]

HECUBA: Agamemnon,
the general of this army that has burned my home to the ground?

TALTHYBIUS: I understand
your feelings.
I understand
this is sudden, and rude.
These days war is so unsparing.

Once upon a time
men fought by day
and grieved at night;
they had the opportunity to consider
the world that they were making;
but now they fight both day and night,
it leaves no time for grief
and so men have come to adopt a certain hardness
that never leaves them
even when the shooting stops.

HECUBA: Yes.
To be sure.
And my son's wife Andromache?

TALTHYBIUS: She is to be taken as wife by the son of Achilles, Neoptolemus.

HECUBA: The son of Achilles.

It's true,
there was once a time

when you came indoors from the fields
you would expect to see
traces of human occupation everywhere:
fires still burning in the fireplaces
because someone meant to come right back,
a book lying face down on the window seat,
a paintbox
and beside it
a glass
full of cloudy water,
flowers in a cut glass vase,
an unfinished game of solitaire,
a piece of cross-stitching
with a needle and thread stuck in it,
building blocks
or lead soldiers
in the middle of the library floor,
lights left burning in empty rooms.
This was the inner life,
not found in great events.
This was the inner life
at home
that's now gone forever.
Men waste so much.
Life is difficult,
I think,
because men don't know the importance of it.

[*She sinks to the ground again.*]

[ANDROMACHE *emerges slowly from the huddled women, wearing torn Lager-feld clothes, holding by one arm a dead doll that she treats with absent-minded casualness, letting it dangle at her side. The doll, a boy, is dressed in a little white jacket (dirtied), white short pants, white shoes. Andromache is beautiful, remote, disconnected, a blown mind—not superficial or silly, but blown away and in shock. There is soft piano music playing.*]

ANDROMACHE: Some days
I remember what it's been like

on a summer day
when the weather's so hot
you can't think what to do with yourself.
You keep waving your fan
but there isn't a breath of fresh air.
And then, just as you're thinking
to put your hand in a bowl of iced water
suddenly:
a letter arrives,
written on a sheet of fine
brilliant red paper
attached to an orchid in full bloom
and you think
how deeply your friend must feel
to have taken such trouble
on a suffocating day

HECUBA [*Going to embrace Andromache*]: Andromache, dear, come to me.
Come.

ANDROMACHE: Suddenly there came a flash of light. And then, I felt some hot
mass attacking me all of a sudden. I felt hot. I lay flat on the ground, trying to
escape the heat. I forgot all about my children for a moment. Then, there
came a big sound.

And you think:
just when I was in such despair
because my garden is torn up
all the flowers torn up
and trampled
all the flowers
that you've come to think are
the most delicate parts of your own body.

HECUBA: Come.
Compose yourself.

ANDROMACHE: These living things
you've cared for,

lying dead
cut open
crushed and trampled on.

The flash was so bright, ten or a hundred or a thousand times brighter than a
camera flash. It pierced my eyes, and my mind went blank. White clouds
spread over the sky. It was as if blue morning-glories had suddenly bloomed
up in the sky.

I think
you can't bring this sort of thing inside
people have Sister Parish do their living rooms
with flowered sofas
and flowered draperies at the windows
and they can be torn down, too
ripped and burned.
You think
well
I deserved it
living all this time in such comfort
when you look around you
and you see others not so well off as you are
suffering
in fact
suffering.

I remember there were Friday night dances
at the golf club,
and Aunt Rose would drive over in her little blue car
and look in on us,
very unobtrusively,
to see how we were doing.
The next
day some of us probably would get some coaching from her
about dancing.
I had my heels going in some funny way,
and she'd give me a demonstration of how I looked
and how to correct it.
The boys would be pumping their dates' arms,

and she'd show them how to dance smoothly.
Bobby was a terrible dancer for a while.
He not only pumped, he hopped.
Joe was probably even worse.
He danced like a longshoreman.
Aunt Rose tried to show him
and then gave up
and made him go to dancing classes.

And what, after all, is my reward
for having been a good wife
a reputation
that some foreigners think I'll make a perfect slave
Not to say I haven't had a wonderful life
a life of privilege.
other people would envy it
even though
it had none of the glamor of Helen's life.

HECUBA: Andromache, we have a full share of today's sorrow
without borrowing from a day long gone. . . .

ANDROMACHE: Every diet I've ever been on
I think I've entered in the proper frame of mind.
And every morning at the clinic
I had an hour of acupuncture
and the needles would be left in
for the whole session while I did my relaxation.
The enemas were a Saturday routine,
and I think my eating habits
underwent a revolution.

Just the other day my trainer said to me
well,
you're in the final weeks of a battle
that has been going on for a long time
and it seems you're going to win most
if not all that you set out to.
You'll be allowed to keep

almost all the new territory and authority
that you've won for yourself
over the last year or two
and it will be seen by others as your property.

[*She has begun to weep.*]

And what will please you even more
is you won't have to give up anything you started with.
That precious home base
that you were willing to die to defend
is safe.
So the net result is that you've extended
what you can call your own.
Of course,
there may still be some last minute concessions
to the other side to be made
but in general you seem to have proved
you can have your cake and eat it.

[*Sobbing*]

The world now sees you
as a force to be reckoned with
not only in your career
but most significantly
in your personal relationships as well.
So, while I stayed home
a faithful wife
well
when it comes down to it
we all make our bargains
although Helen knew right from the start
you might as well take the risk
knowing how it will end in any case.
So she ends up with a nasty reputation
but a good life.

HECUBA: Andromache . . .

ANDROMACHE: I can't help myself from thinking
too
if I'd known
there were other things I meant to get
things I would have liked
if I'd known it was going to end so soon.

When I was a girl
I had a horse I loved so much
I wanted to take him right inside me
or suck his cock.
And I would have done it, too,
if I hadn't been so timid.

Or I'd have hung myself in the bathroom.
Things I didn't do because I was afraid
put a rope around your neck
to get a more intense feeling
you know
cross-dress
wear pants and a necktie
stand on a chair and hang from something.
I was always afraid I'd slip and fall
but when you think about it now
I might as well have run the risk.
Or had myself wrapped up in Saran wrap
I always thought it would be just like a cocoon
covered up and warm
helpless and exposed
all at once.
Or have a man kiss me
between my legs
while he had ice cubes in his mouth.

HECUBA: Andromache, dear, this is not the company for such talk . . .

ANDROMACHE: But, no,
you think,
you musn't put a drink to your lips
when you have food in your mouth

or you may leave a particle of food in your drink
or make a mark on the rim of your glass.
Or, if you bring a piece of food to your mouth with your fork
it is thought nowadays that the tines should be pointing down, not up.
One musn't dunk a donut or a cookie in public.
Nothing may be spit out,
however surreptitiously, into a napkin,   .
not even a bad clam.
Olives are put all at once into the mouth.
Would you sign a letter Mrs. R. C. Jones?
No.
Or Mrs. Robert Jones?
No.
You would sign it with your maiden name
or your married name,
such as Marion Jones
and then, in parentheses,
if the person to whom the letter is addressed doesn't know this,
one could write Mrs. R. C. Jones.

[*A telephone rings throughout the following.*]

And a widow,
if she wishes,
may entertain a gentleman friend for a weekend
if she is more than 30 years of age
and if her children are present in the house
although every woman
should value her reputation
and conduct herself in such a way
that she does not make a public display
of her very private life.

CHEA: It must be a shock for a woman in your position
to be treated this way

EISA: A thing to be used to sweep the floor
and thrown away when it's worn out.

CHEA: Nothing new to us of course.

EISA: Now you see,
the haves are the ones who have their own bodies
and the have nots don't
I'm not surprised it escaped your notice.

VALERIE: Have some pity.

EISA [*Looking toward Hecuba and Andromache*]: For them?

VALERIE: Yes.

EISA: Oh, sure, sure,
it's always those who've suffered least
who need a little sympathy:
like men.

[*Silence*]

BILL: Well, you know, I had my ear ripped off.

[*Silence*]

By a woman.

CHEA: Your ear ripped off?

BILL: It was a, like, more of a drunken brawl type thing, and I had a beer bottle smashed across the side of my head, cut my—you know, bottom of my ear lobe off, it was sort of dangling by a piece of skin—and had seventeen staples in the side of my head, too, at the same time. And plus had two thirds of the cornea of my right eye furrowed out by a fingernail.

EISA: What were you . . .

BILL: I was running away from my wife. And so then she stabbed me in the back, too, with a—like, you know—Ginsu-type steak knife. And I have a scar.

[*He starts to pull up his shirt to show a scar.*]

And I love my wife.

RAY BOB: I know what you mean.

BILL: But she eggs me on. I . . .

RAY BOB: Right.

BILL: I mean, I love my wife,
and when she's straight and she's not drinking or taking Valiums or
    anything . . .

RAY BOB: She's a nice person.

BILL: she's the most even-spoken, nicest person in the world.

RAY BOB: Right.

BILL: And I'm the same way. I can't—
I can't throw stones at her.
I've—I used to drink and do cocaine and—
and I've had my wild times.

RAY BOB: But, I mean, when you say you used to do cocaine,
the fact is you've put, basically,
your family fortune up your nose, Bill,
am I right here?

BILL: Pretty much so, yeah. Yeah.

RAY BOB: And isn't that one of the things that so aggravates Janine?

BILL: Right. Sure. I've acknowledged that.
Haven't I acknowledged that?

EISA: Right, right,
okay, but you know,
you're talking to someone who had five husbands
so it's not like I don't know anything about men.

CHEA: Six husbands, I thought you had six husbands.

EISA: Five.
All bad.
I mean with my first husband
all my children were born out of rape.
I never had normal sex with him.

RAY BOB: Your first husbnd was a *rapist*?

EISA: And he beat me.
He used to beat me, that's how he got turned on.
And then he'd rape me.

CHEA: So then you married. . . .

EISA: He used to lock me in a closet while I was pregnant
so no one could see my injuries
because we were stationed in Guantanamo Bay
and he didn't want his—want the other sailors to see my injuries.

CHEA: Okay. So. Go ahead. Husband number two.

EISA: He, well, he, three days after we were married,
he wanted me to get rid of my children.
And he just made a complete change.
The only way he wanted to have sex was anally,
and he lost my money at the race track,
which was supposed to be for a business.

CHEA: Right.

EISA: Put sugar in my car.
Tried to extort money from me,
and everything.

CHEA: Husband number three.

EISA: He married me to get a green card.

CHEA: He was . . . ?

EISA: a man from a foreign country.

AIMABLE: I heard he was a prince from Jordan.

CHEA: Is that true?

EISA: No.
I don't know where that got around.

CHEA: Okay.

EISA: No.

CHEA: Okay. Number four?

EISA: He was an Italian guy I met.
I knew him ten days and he just swooped me off my feet.

CHEA: Unh-hunh.

EISA: And tried to get my home from me
and was beating on me,
very, very abusive.
Turned out he was bisexual and he was—
we were married about ten days.

CHEA: Husband number five we know was Robert Sand,
the man you were convicted of murdering.
And who was number six?

EISA: That was Joe Mims.

SEI: The man you married the day you were indicted . . .

EISA: Right.

SEI: for the murder of your husband.

CHEA: So that's six.

EISA: Oh, right, if you count Joe,
that's six.

SEI: Where is he now?

EISA: He died of a heart attack on the day we were going to get remarried.
So?

CHEA: So nothing.

EISA: So if you want to count him, that's six.

CHEA [*With complete indifference, dropping the conversation*]: That's all I said.

[*Silence.* TALTHYBIUS *notices the doll Andromache holds.*]

TALTHYBIUS: Who is this?

ANDROMACHE: Who?

TALTHYBIUS: This boy you hold.

ANDROMACHE: This is not a boy.
This is a doll.

TALTHYBIUS: Is this your son?

ANDROMACHE: Astyanax?

TALTHYBIUS: I thought all the men of the royal family were dead.

ANDROMACHE: They are.

TALTHYBIUS: Except this one it seems.
A living heir to the throne.

ANDROMACHE: This one, too, is dead.

TALTHYBIUS: What are you saying?
Are you saying it's a doll
or are you saying that it's dead?

ANDROMACHE: I'm saying both.

TALTHYBIUS: Do you think I can make sense of that?

ANDROMACHE: It's not my business what you can make sense of.

TALTHYBIUS: Which is it?
Is it a doll, or is it dead?

ANDROMACHE: It's mine.
I'm saying it's mine.
What do you care why I have it?
It's mine to keep.

TALTHYBIUS [*To Bill*]: Take the boy with you.

ANDROMACHE: No!

[BILL *snatches the doll from Andromache and knocks her to the ground with a savage hit, so that she falls like a rock. The entire* CHORUS *falls suddenly to the ground, and* HECUBA *stands by astonished.*]

HECUBA [*Going slowly to the ground, embracing Andromache*]: Andromache, my child

ANDROMACHE: My child gone.
They've taken my child.

When they came the first time,
I think I must have been
down already
crawling on all fours

thinking only of myself again

I heard a shot
Blood splashed on my head and neck
I pretended I was dead
Some men came to see
if anyone was moving

I had to stop myself from shivering
I felt a boot kick my side
They spat on the bodies and walked away
And then I forgot entirely
I had been lying on top of my son
to protect him from the gunfire
I still held his hand
I'd kept him with me all that time
like a bird underneath his mother's wing
But now, what difference has it made?
I let my attention wander
for just a moment.
And now he's gone.
They've taken him.

[*Hecuba holds Andromache, comforting her.*]

HECUBA: Sometimes, when you were a child
you would come to my bed when there was a storm.
The storm would rage all night,
the wind knocking branches from the trees,
or even worse,
it would tear out a whole tree and throw it to the ground.
And we would wake in the morning, you and I,
and look out through the lattice,
feeling so sad
to see such disarray—
leaves blown across the ground,
branches and lawn chairs scattered everywhere,
flowers twisted and gnarled—
and then, as though on purpose,
the wind would blow gently through the lattice,
and it would be hard to believe
this was the same wind
that just last night
had raged so violently.

[*Cassandra enters running at top speed—maybe opening with a hostile,
aggressive song.*

She is wearing black. A very chic—though torn—outfit from Comme les Garçons.]

CASSANDRA: Am I too late?

TALTHYBIUS: What?

CASSANDRA: Have I missed the wedding?

BILL: Who is this?

HECUBA [*calling out as though to warn her*]: Cassandra!

TALTHYBIUS: Is this Cassandra?

CASSANDRA: The bride of Agamemnon!
And blessed am I to lie at a king's side.

[*She throws herself at Talthybius's feet.*]

I who see the future:
I see no future for you.

And I'll tell you what I see
in this king Agamemnon's future:
I see he takes a bride
who will climb into his bed
and cut his throat.

HECUBA: No, child, don't.

RAY BOB: She's nothing but trouble this one.

CASSANDRA: Not for me
the life of mourning.

EISA: No.

HECUBA: Cassandra, have some sense
of the position you find yourself in now.

These men are not your brothers
you may tease
and expect them to forgive . . .

TALTHYBIUS: I must say,
to speak
not so much as a diplomat
but as a . . .

CASSANDRA [*to Talthybius*]: One day, when I lie dead cold and naked
next to my husband's tomb
piled in a ditch for animals to rip and feed on
beaten by the storms of winter,
you, too, you will be lying in some mud pit
or buried
somewhere no one will remember
or give a shit
what you've done long since forgotten
unless some bitch strings you up
before that
with hoods and gags and blindfolds

HECUBA: Cassandra . . .

TALTHYBIUS: I beg your . . .

CASSANDRA: and you feel some dizziness coming on

EISA: some nausea

CASSANDRA: some chick's getting her rocks off
cutting you up a little bit
plugging you into the wall
cranking you up on the rheostat?

[*All the women speaking at once over each other. It moves with dizzying speed.*]

EISA: putting a long pin through his flesh and scraping his bones

CHEA: sewing his lips together,

EISA: sewing his eyelids open,

CHEA: sewing his hands together

EISA: nailing his scrotum to a chair

CASSANDRA: Not that *all* these assholes shouldn't be eliminated
these dicks with their pussy envy

HECUBA: Darling,
these men have power to dispose of all of us—
not you alone
but your sisters, too,
and me as well.
Think of your sisters if not of yourself;
don't invite the cruelty of these men just now.

[*Cassandra's attention is momentarily distracted by her mother.*]

CHEA: These cuntsuckers

EISA: these pricks who can only compensate
for not being a woman
by savaging some entire country

CASSANDRA: It doesn't follow
because men have always been around
like a disease
that they always must be around
because these men are not needed!

CHEA: We can make whole human beings
in laboratories.

CASSANDRA: I've loved a man
I know what it is to love.
A man whose kisses were so sweet,
so much of a different time.

[*Hecuba has buried herself again in the pile of rags.*]

We might be loved for a while and then forgotten.
But the love will have been enough;
all those impulses of love return to the love that made them.
Even memory is not necessary for love.
There is a land of the living
and a land of the dead,
and the bridge is love,
the only meaning.

Let's have him, then,
Bring me to him.
Take me into his home.
Let me lie down with him
stretch him out on a board
put weights on his chest.
Is this a man who likes to be bitten
all over his body
on his neck and chest?
Does he like to be laced
with needle and thread
like a spider's web
sewn down to his bed
immobilized?
Then he's chosen well
which woman here
to take back home with him.

Where is this general's ship?
Take me to it,
and know, that when this ship leaves the shore
it carries with it
one of the Furies.

[*The* CHORUS, *led by* CASSANDRA, *sings a song.*

At the end of the song, CASSANDRA *runs out at full tilt.*]

HECUBA: Come back!
Stop her, someone.
She doesn't know what she's saying.
She doesn't mean it.

TALTHYBIUS: I had hoped we could proceed with some sense of self-respect
but I see this is not to be the case.
Where is your daughter Polyxena?

HECUBA: Polyxena?
She found a ship.
She's run away.
She's gone.

TALTHYBIUS: We know she's here.

HECUBA: She's a child,
a young child.

TALTHYBIUS: It's been decided she should be given to Achilles.

HECUBA: Achilles?

TALTHYBIUS: Yes.

HECUBA: Achilles is dead.

TALTHYBIUS: Yes.
It's true he's dead,
His companions in arms
have decided
that his body cannot be left here in Troy
in an unhonored grave.

HECUBA: Unhonored?

TALTHYBIUS: Achilles was a hero.
His companions remember his courage in battle.
How he went in where others were afraid
with no care for his own safety

as though he were already dead.
So.
His fellow soldiers will not see him buried
without a proper sacrifice
to give honor to his sacrifice.
Just as all the living will be given companions
he, too, must have a companion in his death.

HECUBA: A young girl to be his companion in death?

TALTHYBIUS: Yes.

HECUBA: After the war is over
and the city lies in ashes
to search out a girl
and kill her, too.

BILL: You keep saying the war is *over.*
But the men are still on *fire,*
their blood racing.
Let's face it:
they'd like to feel
the impact of two or three more bombs exploding,
the woods moving like one living creature
heaving up the earth,
the slow collapsing pull of gravity,
before they feel at peace.

TALTHYBIUS: I am not the man to do this,
I admit it.
Some other,
without pity,
should have come in my place.
But I've come to do my job.

HECUBA: To do your job?
What about my job?
I've not yet finished raising these children.
My mother said to me,
a gentleman is one who considers not just another's rights

but also her preferences.
I've not finished teaching my children
about the sacredness of human life.
This is my work.

Let me keep my daughter Polyxena,
my youngest child,
only Polyxena.
Or, if you must have someone to put atop Achilles' grave,
take me instead.

[POLYXENA, *who had been hiding among the members of the chorus, steps forward. She is 13 years old, funkily dressed in torn jeans and a tarty looking red velvet bustier (not that she is tarty, but that that is the—unconscious?—teen-age style).*]

POLYXENA: No.
Take me.
Here I am.

HECUBA: Go back!

POLYXENA: I'm not afraid.
I heard everything.
Don't be afraid, mother.
[*To Talthybius*]
You won't take her.
I'm going with you.

HECUBA: No.
[*She goes to Polyxena and holds her.*]
She's a child.

POLYXENA: I don't feel sorry, mother,
it's my fate.
If you have an eight for a name
then you can have an eight and a four
or an eight and a thirteen
you come to combinations of twenty-one,
or three

you know then that's your fate.
I might have had a nine
but if you believe in numerology
you know you don't choose your numbers
they're given to you
and you learn to accept them.

HECUBA: She doesn't mean what she's saying.
She's a child.

POLYXENA: Yes, I do.
I think
I wish I had lived to have some years with you
when we would both be grown-ups
and talk as equals
and share our thoughts.

[*Breaking loose from Hecuba*]

But when it's in your numbers
or your horoscope
you just know
that's the way the world was
when you had your life
and you accept it.

Of course, I have to admit
I'd have liked to live a little longer
I mean there's a lot I don't know yet.
Like: why do guys insist on driving?
And how come they call on Friday to ask you out
for Friday night?
And why do guys hate to get dressed up?
How come they don't like to talk on the phone?
Why do guys drink out of the milk carton?
And how come they like to play air guitar?
Why is a guy who sleeps around a stud
but a girl who does is a slut?

BILL: I think it's almost expected of a guy.

POLYXENA: How come guys wait till way after they love you
to say they do?

TALTHYBIUS: It's nervousness, I think.

POLYXENA: And why is it they keep on checking out other girls
even though they insist you're the only one?

VALERIE: It's just human nature to look at beautiful girls.
It doesn't necessarily mean anything at all.

POLYXENA: How can a guy stand to make out with a girl
he makes fun of to his friends?

RAY BOB: It's just peer pressure.
It's a bad thing to do,
but if a guy's friends start making fun of the girl,
it's easier to go along with the crowd.
He doesn't mean it.

POLYXENA: And how come they don't like to fight?

RAY BOB: They're afraid they'll say something they didn't mean to say,
because sometimes they don't think so fast,
and they'll get dumped.

POLYXENA: How come they back off as soon as they know you like them?

VALERIE: They're scared.

POLYXENA: Guys need so much space.
A few months ago,
I had sex with my cousin.
We've never talked about it since.

[*Polyxena sings, and then, after the song:*]

POLYXENA: I guess, when you think of having regrets,
I regret we never talked about it.

HECUBA: Let my child stay with me.
This is a good child.
Let her stay with me.

[RAY BOB *and* BILL *take hold of Polyxena and throw Hecuba to the ground.*]

POLYXENA: Mother!

HECUBA: No! No!

[RAY BOB *wraps a scarf around Polyxena's mouth and hustles her off the stage.*
TALTHYBIUS *and* BILL *follow.*

Through the following song, no one speaks.
They all look at the door through which Polyxena was taken.
Andromache goes to the door, stops, looks
turns away, walks away,
turns back, walks toward the door, stops, looks,
turns away, walks away, stops, turns back to look,
starts to walk toward the door, stops, looks.]

The CHORUS *sings "Calling All Angels," from Wim Wenders film* Until the End
of the World.

HECUBA *is still collapsed on the ground.* MENELAUS *enters. He wears a torn military uniform. His hair is matted with blood. And as the scene goes on, his uniform oozes blood. He speaks to a chorus member.*]

MENELAUS: I beg your pardon.
I am looking for Helen,
my wife.

HECUBA: Menelaus?

MENELAUS: Yes.

EISA: You're the man responsible
for this war?

MENELAUS: So they say.

CHEA: Because you couldn't keep your wife at home.

MENELAUS: I love her.

HECUBA: For that you took thousands to their death.

MENELAUS: A war begun
by a friend of mine,
a countryman of yours,
welcomed into my home as a guest
who took my wife
in violation of my trust.

Took my wife.

Raped my wife.

CHEA: Your wife was taken from you?

MENELAUS: Yes.

CHEA: This is not the story that we heard.

MENELAUS: Stolen.

EISA: We were told she ran away from you.

MENELAUS: Really.
Put it how you will.
My friend betrayed me.
Or my wife did.
Broke her promise.
Her vow of marriage.
Betrayed my love.
That's the point, isn't it?

In marriage,
and in the world.
If we betray our trust,
we *are* at war.

A society at peace
is founded on mutual promises,
freely given
without coercion.
And when such promises are broken,
when one party
on its own,
decides to enforce its preference
by some unilateral action
then if the relationship continues
it is based upon coercion,
then force has come into play,
war has been declared.

And then?
And then, when my friend
was asked to bring my wife back to me,
he was instead supported by all his countrymen
in his act.
So that they,
you,
became accomplices in this betrayal of love and trust,
this destruction of the foundation of my life,
and of my society.

You and your friends
treated with contempt
that mutual trust that is essential
for my country
to live with itself
in peace.

You violated our peace.
And so we have annihilated yours.
And would do it again.

Now, I've come for my wife.
I know she is inside here.
My friends,
the victors in this war,

have given her to me
to bring her home with me,
or not
as I will.

CHEA: Chattel, like the rest of us.

MENELAUS [*To another chorus member*]: Who is this person?
[*To Chea*]
I said she is my wife.
I said: I'll have her back.

The truth is I can sleep in a bed of ice if I choose;
I can detach my head
and let it trundle off somewhere on its own.
At times I feel myself going down
a steep and winding staircase to a bottomless depth,
but I look with wonder at my hands from time to time
when they've gone numb.
They'll do anything I like:
take my cock in one hand
and rub it on your bellies
and hang you on a peg
to cut you open.
Do you think if I cut the artery in your neck
you'd spurt blood?
I'll have her back
or kill you
one by one
until I've cleared my path to her.

But sometimes I like to lie down at night
with my arms around someone
and *know* she loves me
know this gives her pleasure—
just lying there
my arms around her
her back to me
my stomach pressed against her back

my face buried in her hair
my arms around her
one hand on her stomach
trusting her love
feeling at peace.

I'll have her back.

Bring her to me.
I want her arms tied behind her back
and I want her dragged to me.

CHEA: Take her back, then.
And when you take her back then:
kill her!

HECUBA: No!

MENELAUS: What?

CHEA: Kill her—
she who brought all this down on us:
kill her,
and we will bless you for it.

EISA: But don't bring her out here.
Have her taken somewhere to be killed
so you don't see her first.
Because we know about you.
You can't look at her without wanting her.

[HELEN *suddenly appears from among the chorus members. She wears a chemise, and nothing else, from Victoria's Secret. She is the seductive survivor, the master of "feminine wiles" (not used by any of the other women in the play) to be used to survive in a man's world.*

The CHORUS *sings the Bow Wow Wow version of "I Want Candy."*

HELEN *continues to sing until she notices Menelaus.*]

HELEN: Menelaus!
Thank God.
I've found you at last.

MENELAUS: Helen . . .

HELEN: Where have you been?
I know.
I know you must hate me.
But, Menelaus,
I've never loved anyone but you.
[*She cries.*]
I couldn't help myself.

CHEA: Tears.

HELEN [*Overlooking the interruption, not responding to it*]: If you want to
    blame someone, blame her!
[*Gesturing to Hecuba*]
She mothered the man who stole me from you.
She raised him,
taught him how to treat a woman.
If Troy is ruined now
she has no one to blame but herself.

Am I to blame for my beauty?

[*The members of the chorus exchange glances;
Helen takes them in,
is distracted momentarily.*]

Am I responsible for how I look?

[*Full attention back to Menelaus*]

Or if you say, well,
nonetheless,

you did run away

hadn't you gone to Crete?
And left me alone in the house in Sparta?

To wonder if you were finished with me?
Do you think . . .
all those years that I loved you . . .
was I not supposed to feel . . .
left alone as I was . . .
was I not supposed to fear . . .
that I would never know your love again?

CHEA: Of course, without a man,
some women would rather have a dildo
than go with the enemy.

SEI: A dildo?

HELEN [*Seizing attention again*]: Do you know,
as soon as Paris was killed in the war,
I tried to find my way back to you.
These women can attest.
But they caught me—
and took me to Dei . . . Dei . . .

CHEA: Deiphobus.

HELEN: Deiphobus,
my second husband . . .
[*Silence*]
who kept me as his wife

[*Looks at chorus, then back to Menelaus*]

by force.

[*Silence, taking in chorus again*]

And now you would kill me?
I
who have been a bride of force.

Do you not think I've suffered enough,
away from you,
that you couldn't bring me back to your bed,
forgive me
lie with me
our arms around each other
to make love
or not
just lie together
your arms around me
your stomach pressed into my back
your arms around me
your face buried in my hair
one hand on my stomach
feeling once again
at peace?

VALERIE: Menelaus, don't be taken in by this.

CHEA: She should be flogged.
She should be caned

SEI: Rule number one: exciting women can make men miserable.

AIMABLE: Rule number two: there are no perfect women.

SEI: Rule number three: reforming a woman is usually futile.

EISA: Rule number four: no woman can give a man self-esteem.

AIMABLE: Rule number five: many good women go unnoticed.

VALERIE: Rule number six: women like men who like women.

AIMABLE: Rule number seven: men who really listen are irresistible.

MENELAUS [*Holding up a hand*]: Enough.
I think I understand my own wife.

CHEA: Then let her be stoned to death now.
There's no one left alive
who wouldn't be eager to help.

HELEN [*Falling to the ground, embracing Menelaus's knees*]: How could this
be?
To have me stoned to death by these *strangers*?
Take me home to Greece, please.
If I must die,
then let me die at home.

CHEA: Put her on the same ship home with you?
She'll have you in her bed in no time.

MENELAUS [*To Chea*]: What do you mean?

VALERIE: A man like you
once in love
will never let a woman go.

[*Silence*]

MENELAUS: I'll take her home.
The others will be back for the rest of you.

[HELEN *and* MENELAUS *sing a duet.*

They turn to leave together.
HELEN *stops, turns back to chorus.*]

HELEN: And you,
you worthless pieces of shit,
don't give me any of your fucking attitude,
try to cut me down
with your whining
oh, here come tears:
blame him,
"she should be flogged,"
"she should be caned,"

these are the seven rules for women and men—
as though you knew your ass from your elbow.
You haven't been anywhere.
You use a fucking dildo,
you fucking
losers.

[*She wheels around and exits with Menelaus.*

Music, very sad, comes up, almost inaudibly at first.

Two chorus women bring in body of Polyxena to Hecuba, who makes her ready for burial.]

SEI: Hecuba
they've let us bring your child to you
to prepare her body to lie atop Achilles' grave.

HECUBA: Polyxena?
Prepare her body?
Oh, no, my child, my child.

[*She buries her head in Polyxena's body, then after a time looks up.*]

How was she put to death?
Tell me.
Let me hear it all.

[*Uncertainty among the chorus members about whether to tell the story; finally one speaks.*]

AIMABLE: The whole army of the Greeks
was drawn up in ranks.
Some soldiers held her arms,
and Achilles' son, Neoptolemus, led her to his father's grave
and there drew his sword to kill her.
But she spoke first:
Wait, she said,
let no man touch me
I die of my own free will,

and the soldiers let her go.
She took hold of her robe at the shoulder
and ripped it open to her waist
She sank to her knees
and said to Neoptolemus,
Here is my breast, then,
will you stab me here?
Here is my throat ready for your sword.
And Neoptolemus,
torn between pity and duty,
stood hesitating
and then, at last,
slashed her throat with his sword
and even as she dropped to the ground
she did so with dignity and grace.

HECUBA: Oh, my child,
this goes past all endurance.

I should have died long ago
but I was kept alive
saved to witness more,
more beyond endurance.
Until now
I myself
finally feel
this rage of war
deep within my own self.
How can I live now
as though all the world's suffering
were only meant to help me
achieve an understanding
for my own edification!
No.
This pain must be answered with more pain,
this brutality with brutality in kind.

Bring Aeneas to me.

SEI: He is afraid . . .

HECUBA: Bring him to me!

We are nothing but creatures waiting
to be shattered by our lives.

In the end,
we don't come through life
as we come through each experience along the way—
wiser, more humane, hardened,
wounded or restored;
in the end we are all
simply
consumed by life.

Now, soon,
all my world will be blotted out with ash.

[*Aeneas enters.*
He is in shock
and is brought in supported, almost carried, by chorus members.
He wears tennis whites that are filthy and torn.
He is completely freaked out, eyes darting, disoriented as though he has just
*   come out of darkness into the light, terrified.*]

AENEAS: Queen Hecuba.

[*He falls to his knees.*]

HECUBA: Stand up.
Your time of hiding is at an end.

AENEAS: Hiding, no, I haven't been . . .

HECUBA: No, not hiding.

AENEAS: No.

HECUBA: Cowering,
while all the other men were murdered
and all the women beaten, raped,

murdered, taken into slavery.
In all this time,
you have been cowering.

[*Silence*]

Now, you see,
here is Polyxena in my arms,
a child,
who did not shrink from death as you did.
Look at her.
Look.
Remember her.

[*Aeneas goes to his knees,*
weeping,
puts his head down on the lifeless body of Polyxena.]

Your time has come to avenge her death.

Learn from this.
See the world
and the men and women who live in it
for what they are.

AENEAS: Right.
I'm not a child, you know.
After the things I've lived to see.

This boy
one time
jumped down out of a truck
thinking he'd be smart,
and he said
Hey,
has anyone ever escaped from here?
So they stripped him naked
and hung him upside down for a few hours,
and then they got him down and laid him on the ground
and poked sand down his throat until he died.

Or you hear the rules that have been set:
anyone who walks away too quickly is shot,
anyone out of line is shot,
anyone who walks too slowly is shot,
anyone who speaks too loudly,
anyone who bends down,
anyone who turns his head,
any child who cries

a hospital floor cleared
by pushing the wheelchairs out on the balcony
tipping the people out of them
into the trucks in the street below

people who have suffocated
their tongues stuck out of their mouths
like dead fish
so that you feel nothing for them so much as
contempt

When I see a girl being drowned
I go crazy
and I have butterflies in my stomach
and pressure of some kind in my temples
and they seem to get hot
I sometimes smell something burning
and I am overcome by panic
I feel some kind of feeling in my penis
my heart rate goes up
I sweat sometimes
I get the runs
and then I masturbate over and over and over and over again
six times a day for days
while I see in my mind the drowning I have seen on television
I wish I could have videotaped it
and watched it over and over again
I have the head rush of that sweeping liquid-like feeling
that goes through my brain when I see a drowning
and I have trouble breathing

I have asthma
I have to use my inhaler to breathe normally again
I might not sleep for days on end
I am in a constant state of fear and agitation
I can't eat
I ache all over
and all because of the drowning of the girl
that I saw on television

VALERIE: This is how men are.

HECUBA: Then make good use of it.
Your time has come
to find all those who have survived,
take them to a new country.
Put your trust in power alone.

Make a nation that can endure.

And when you have,
come back,
reduce these Greeks and their world
to ash.
Ruin their cities.
Burn them.
Pull down their homes.
Leave not one stone standing on another.
Let them die of their wounds alone and abandoned.
Let them bleed to death on their own graves.

Go now.
Leave Troy.
Find some other place to gather your strength for your return.
Take whom you can and go.

Have you heard me?

AENEAS: Yes.

HECUBA: Do you hear me?
No more hiding!
Be a man!

AENEAS: I will.
You can count on me.

HECUBA: What other men are here?
Come out now.
No more hiding.
It's safe to come out.
Where are you?

[*One or two men come out from rocks or crevices or other hiding places, looking sheepish.*]

Here you are.

AENEAS: Any others!
Come on out,
let's go.

Come with me.

HECUBA: You've given me your word.
Don't forget.

AENEAS: I won't.
You can count on me.

[*Aeneas turns and leaves—followed out by eight or ten men who gradually—sheepishly—scurry out of the places they have been hiding all this time.*

At the very end, one of the men who has been dressed as a woman and hiding in the chorus, takes off his wig and goes with the men.

Hecuba remains with Polyxena in her arms, rocking back and forth with her for a long, long time, while we hear a song.]

THE MUSICAL

Characters
CHORUS OF WOMEN, including

    ANDREA

    CAROL

    ALICE

    LETTY

FOUR VETERANS

    JOE

    JIM

    EDDIE

    AENEAS

DIDO (might be double cast as Helen)

Carthage

A bright full moon in a deep blue sky

The dramaturgical rules have shifted here:
this is dreamland, a world of drift, heaven.

A spa
Exercise machines of all sorts
Bowls of fruit
Bottles of Evian water
Fresh flowers
Piles of towels
A hot tub

Women are working out on these machines.
This is the chorus: they are, variously,
patrons and instructors at the spa.

These are not the same women as are in the Prologue.

They turn to face the audience, even as they continue their workouts, and sing.

[THE VETERANS *step tentatively into the room.*]

JOE: Excuse me.
I'm sorry.

[*The women turn, surprised to see the men there.*]

I apologize,
but . . .
is this a club for women only?

ANDREA: No.

CAROL: Well, yes it is.

ANDREA: Come in.

ALICE: Come in.

LETTY: What's happened to you?

JOE: We've been . . .
uh . . .

JIM: Beaten.
In war.
Routed.

JOE: Thrown out.

EDDIE: Exiled.

JOE: From our home.

JIM: Troy.

ALICE: You're refugees.

JOE: Yes.

JIM: From the war in Troy.

EDDIE: We're pacifists, really.

LETTY: Well, come in.
Come.

[*She opens her arms to them.*]
You're safe here.

JOE: Thank you.

JIM: Where are we?

EDDIE: I think we've died and gone to heaven,
if you ask me.

JOE: This is Rome, right?
Is this Rome?

ANDREA: No.

JIM: I thought we were going to Rome.
Where are we?

ALICE: This is Carthage.

JOE: Carthage?

EDDIE: Where is Carthage?

JIM: Is this on the way to Rome?

ANDREA: If that's where you're going.

JIM: We've been at sea for
I don't know
a week, ten days.
Coming from—well . . .
Do you know where Troy is?

ALICE: No.

JIM: It's . . . uh . . .
where is it?

JOE: East.
It's east of here.
Or north.
I don't know
it seems like, what,
ten day?

JIM: By ship.

JOE: Of course, we had some bad winds.

EDDIE: Well, and we had,
you know,
a bad war.
I mean everyone getting killed.

JIM [*He begins to get speedy.*]: every day getting up not knowing where they'd
come from,
you find some guy who'd been your best friend
suddenly dead lying there next to you.

JOE [*Sharply, bringing him back to consciousness*]: That's enough.

JIM: Right. Right.
That's all over.

JOE: That's where we came from.
We're a little—still—

JIM: On edge . . .

JOE: Not quite ourselves.

EDDIE: Is this a . . . you know . . .
Is this a feminine utopia?

ANDREA: No.
This is a gym.

EDDIE: Oh.
A gym.
Right.
OK then.
A gym.

Because I don't see any guys.

JIM: Or a spa.
More like a spa.

ANDREA: Right.

JOE: It's nice.

EDDIE: Are there . . . uh . . .
I mean:
You know, are there any men here?

ALICE: The men are gone.

JOE: Gone.

ANDREA: They went to war.

JOE: Where?

ALICE: In Libya.

EDDIE: Where is that?

ANDREA: West of here.

JOE: And they didn't come back.

ALICE: Right.

JIM: They were all killed, you mean.

ANDREA: Right.

JOE: I'm sorry.

JIM: Like us.

EDDIE: Except we weren't killed.

JOE: And we didn't go to war.
Like, the war came to us.

JIM: Right.
And, plus, we weren't all killed.

[*Silence*]

Do you miss them?

ANDREA [*Simply—no great tragedy*]: Well, sure.

EDDIE: I like it here.

[*Silence*]

JIM [*To Alice*]: I like women.

ANDREA: Do you?
What is it you like about women?

[*During the following exchanges, the women move to the men, put their arms
around them comfortingly, help them toward massage tables and recliner chairs.*

*None of the following remarks are lascivious, even those of Jim; they are deliv-
ered gently—as memories of gentler days—and taken as such by the women.*]

JIM: Oh, well, I like—
you know, to be honest,
I like the way they feel.
I mean,
I like the way they *are*, too,

and the way they sound
and what they say.
I mean,
I guess all women don't say the same thing exactly.

ALICE
Right.

JIM: But there's a certain
thing
I mean: among *some* women,
a kind of gentleness.
I mean, of course, they can be tough, too.
that's okay, that could even be good.
I'm not . . . you know . . .
but I like the way women usually are,
or they have this, you know, basic thing—
and I like the way they smell
you know.

ALICE: Some women . . .

JIM: Right.
And how a woman can just: take more in than a man,
I mean, in a way,
be more open, or
you know, I think women are smart,
how they don't exclude stuff
that men sometimes have to, you know, exclude
or else they get too confused,
you know what I mean?
I mean, most women.

ALICE: And most men.

JIM: Right.

The truth is: there are times I feel I could kiss a woman's cheek for hours and
hours at a time, nestle my face in her hair, whisper in her ear.

JOE: I love to kiss a woman's ear.
In fact, to tell the truth,
I like to crawl right up inside a woman.

JIM: I like to hold a woman,
have a woman hold me.

JOE: I like to put my head on a woman's breast
have her arms around me
so that I can't escape
and fall asleep.

JIM: Sometimes I think of having my head on a woman's breast
and then I think of her head on my chest
and my mind goes back and forth
back and forth
I can't settle on one thought or the other
I love them both so much.

JOE: I like to see a woman smile.
I love it when a woman laughs

JIM: Following her thoughts
while she tells a story
where she goes
where her voice is quiet or deep
where she hesitates
where she stops
where she takes a long slow curve
where she takes a quick turn without thinking
where she thinks it's funny

EDDIE: I like to get inside a woman's head
as much as in her body.

JIM: I like to dress in her clothes.

JOE: I'd like to be a woman.

[*Aeneas is left back by the chorus, standing alone.*

Music.

From the doors of the sauna at upstage center, DIDO *enters. She looks at Aeneas for a moment, then turns and at once steps directly to the microphone at center stage.*

She sings the Linda Ronstadt arrangment of "When You Wish Upon a Star."

At the end of the song, she fixes Aeneas in her gaze.]

DIDO: What's your name?

AENEAS [*Transfixed*]: Aeneas.

DIDO: You know,
a cave that has been dark for a million years
will become bright
the moment a candle is lit inside it.

Things can happen so suddenly.

AENEAS: Yes.

DIDO: In spring, I think,
the dawn is most beautiful.

AENEAS: Yes.

DIDO: In summer, the nights.

AENEAS: Yes.

DIDO: In autumn, the evenings.

In winter, the early mornings.

AENEAS: Right.

DIDO: Where are you from?

AENEAS: Troy.

DIDO: You're kind of a mess, you know it?

AENEAS: Right. I know,
well, we've been . . .
We're refugees from the war in Troy.

DIDO: I know.
We saw you land.
Where are you going?

AENEAS: I don't know.
Somewhere.
Rome I guess.
We've just stopped here to rest.
Who are you?

DIDO: My name is Dido.
I'm the queen.

AENEAS: What?

DIDO: I'm the queen here.

AENEAS: Right.
I knew that.
I mean—
I've heard about you.

DIDO: What have you heard?

AENEAS: Well, you know,
I don't know—
stuff.
Like:
you're good at crossword puzzles.

DIDO: You heard that?

AENEAS: Word gets out.

DIDO: Well, I've heard about you, too.

AENEAS: I doubt it.

DIDO: Yes. I have.

AENEAS: Like what?

DIDO: I heard you could suck someone's soul out through their eyeballs just by looking at them.

AENEAS: I'm sorry?

DIDO: You hadn't heard that about yourself?

AENEAS: What does that mean?

DIDO: You tell me. You're the one who does it.

AENEAS: I don't think so.

DIDO: You're doing it right now.

AENEAS: I'm sorry.

DIDO: You don't need to apologize.

They say you're a war hero.

AENEAS: Me?
No, no,
I don't think so.
That's not me.
You've got me confused with someone else.

DIDO: Really?

AENEAS: I'm not in such good shape just now.
I don't feel too good about how I've been,
you know,
behaving.

DIDO: Really?

AENEAS: You know, right now
I'm just trying to get from day to day.
I brought these guys out with me—
I don't know that I'm up to it
I'm a young man, I guess,
but I'm feeling kind of too old, too—
like the worst of both worlds, you know,
too young to know
and too old to do it if I did know.

DIDO: You need some herbs, probably.

AENEAS: Herbs?

DIDO: Blue-green algae,
something like that.
Do you ever drink ginseng tea?

AENEAS: Ginseng tea? No, I don't think so.

DIDO: Would you like to try it?

AENEAS: Is that what you drink?

DIDO: Sometimes.

AENEAS: I guess I'd like to drink whatever you drink.

[*They sit and have tea together.*]

DIDO: Do you have a girl friend?

AENEAS [*Shock—incredulity—laughter*]: Me?
No.
I guess not.

DIDO: Some women go for wrecked-up guys.

AENEAS: How about you?

DIDO: I don't go for wrecked-up guys.
I go for guys who've been around.
I go for guys who sail boats,
but I'm not drawn to shipwrecked guys, no.

I go for guys who have it together.
I go for guys who feel confident enough
to walk around the house with no clothes on
and let you look at their bodies.

AENEAS: Unh-hunh.

DIDO: When I was in art school
I made this series of sculptures of men
really plaster casts of their torsos, you know what I mean?

AENEAS: What do you mean?

DIDO: Well, you just take wet plaster and put it on somebody
and when you take it off, you have an exact sculpture of them—
you've seen that kind of thing.

AENEAS: I guess so.

DIDO: So I did these guys' torsos
or, their midsections really
from their knees to their chests
wearing blue-jeans but no shirts.
But first, so you can get the plaster off again
you have to smear them with vaseline—
so I'd smear them—

put the vaseline on
and then the plaster,
and the plaster gets very hot while's it's getting hard
and the heat would make it so that—
well, none of the guys could help it—
they all got these incredible erections.
So the whole series of sculptures
were of these guys in blue jeans with incredible erections.
I called it the hard-on series.

How about you?

AENEAS: What?

DIDO: What kind of women do you like?

AENEAS: Oh.
I like a woman who's smart.

[*Silence*]

DIDO: That's it?

AENEAS: Really smart.
I mean really smart.
Like quick.
And alive.
You know: really alert.
I guess, smart in every way.
Really conscious.
Vital, I guess.
You know what I mean?

DIDO: I don't think so.

AENEAS: I like a woman who is so alive
that she jumps when I touch her,
if I touch her, like, in a sensitive place,
I mean touch her gently—
I don't know, am I out of line here?

I mean, I want a woman
who laughs and cries a lot.
I've had friendships with women who have been really passionate
but really crazy
and women who have been really sane
but not so passionate;
and I wish I'd find someone who is really passionate
and really sane both at the same time
and wants a deep, passionate,
one-on-one relationship—
and, you know,
laughs at my jokes
not just out of politeness
but because she thinks they're really funny.

DIDO: Tell me one.

AENEAS: A joke?

DIDO: Yeah.

AENEAS: Well, I don't just tell jokes, like jokes.
It's just sometimes I say things that are funny.

DIDO: On purpose?

AENEAS: Sure.
But,
I guess,
probably not usually.

DIDO: Do you believe in love at first sight?

AENEAS: Sure.

DIDO: Why?

AENEAS: I don't know.
Because, I guess,
I think people really fall in love for stuff that's so deep

and so particular
so specific
like, say, the space that someone's body takes up—
I don't mean like how beautiful they are,
though someone will seem beautiful to you,
or even be beautiful,
but even like how their elbow joints are so pointed
or their shoulder blades are so close together
or exactly that far apart
or their body just—
occupies that space—
or the way they smell, let's face it—
or, you know,
their ankles.
I knew a woman once who was really a wonderful woman—
I mean a remarkable person—
and I just couldn't stand her ankles—
I just held it against her for no reason;
I kept talking to myself
trying to reason with myself
but it was no use.
Or someone might be repulsive in some way
but it doesn't matter
or really stupid or boring but you don't even care
because they, like, have a certain way about them
a kind of openness
or caring quality
warmth, say,
or just passion.
Or maybe the stuff that really matters
is something at a cellular level really
that you don't even know what it is
at a verbal level I mean
but, you know,
you just get—like in three-point-two seconds—
forty-two thousand bits of very specific and irresistible subcellular
    information
that you never know what it is
even if you stay married for fifty years.

Do you?

DIDO: What?

AENEAS: Believe in love at first sight?

DIDO: I think it's the only kind there is.
[*The* WOMEN'S CHORUS *sings a song.*]

DIDO: Have you ever read Tarot cards?

AENEAS: No.

DIDO: Would you like to?

AENEAS: Ummm. Sure.

DIDO: You don't believe in the cards?

AENEAS: Do you?

DIDO: Well, of course I do.

AENEAS: Unh-hunh.

DIDO: So, do you?

AENEAS: Want to read them?

DIDO: Believe in them?

AENEAS: I'd like to read them with you.

[*She takes a deck of tarot cards.*

While Dido and Aeneas do the cards, the VETERANS *serve food and drink to the chorus, make the women comfortable, bring them robes, etc.*]

DIDO: First,
you take the cards

and hold them.
Look at them.
And choose one you like.

AENEAS: One I like?

DIDO: One that feels good to you.

[*He looks through the cards.*]

AENEAS: This one feels pretty good.

DIDO: The three of wands.
A calm person.
Stately.
His back turned.
Standing on the edge of a cliff
looking out to sea at passing ships.
His ships.

Were you thinking of leaving?

AENEAS: Well, no.

DIDO: This guy is standing on the shore
looking at the ships.
With longing, maybe.

AENEAS: Longing for you, maybe.

DIDO: You think I'm a ship?

AENEAS [*Silence*]: Sure.

DIDO: Here.
Let me have the deck.

[*She shuffles them, places one down.*]

This is what you do.
You choose another card.

Like that.
Put it on top of the first.
This covers him.

AENEAS: Covers him?

DIDO: That's what they say.

AENEAS: The Star.

DIDO: This is the influence that works on you now.
Loss. Abandonment.

AENEAS: Really.
I don't think that's me.
Of course, in a way, sure, that's obvious, but . . .

DIDO: Or some would say: it means hope. Bright prospects.

AENEAS: It seems you can say whatever you want.

DIDO: Sort of.
Yeah.
[*She takes another card and puts it down.*]
These are his obstacles.

AENEAS: A dead man?
With ten swords in his back?
No kidding.
That's all for me.

DIDO: You can't stop now.
It's just like life.
Once you start,
you have to see it to the end.

AENEAS: Unh-hunh.
Let's move along a little faster then.
What else have you got here?

[*Beat*]

DIDO: All right.
Here's the page of cups.
Taste.
Seduction.
Deception.

AENEAS: Not deception, no.
Or seduction either.
You don't think I'm seducing *you*, do you?

DIDO: The cards don't lie.
They're only cards after all.

AENEAS: And do you think I would deceive you?

DIDO: Have you ever deceived anyone else?

AENEAS: Recently you mean.

DIDO: I meant ever.

AENEAS: Yes.

DIDO: Then I guess you could deceive me, too.
[*Turning over another card*]
Uh-oh.

AENEAS: The death card probably.

DIDO: No.

Well, yes, it is.

But
it's okay.
It's only cards.

AENEAS: You just said you believe in them.

DIDO: But death, you know,
isn't always bad, either.
I mean, until you die
you can't be reborn.

AENEAS: Unh-hunh.
Look.
Let me have the cards.
You know,
I can read these cards, too.

[*Tossing the cards out quickly, haphazardly*]

Here: the moon.
The moon is change.

So the story begins with change.
And moves back
[*Not even looking at the cards as he tosses them out*]
from the outer cards to the center
through darkness
to intoxication
to giving in to my heart
then to wisdom and happiness
to death
and to rebirth in love
with you.

That's how I read the cards.
What do you think?

[*Long silence*]

DIDO: This wouldn't be fair for you to do, you know,
to make me fall in love with you.
I can tell you how you can read the cards
and leave
keep on going
wherever it was you were going
and I could let you go,

you know, not get anything started,
we just met.

AENEAS: Let's face it.

DIDO: I am facing it.
Face what?

AENEAS: You see what's in the cards—
I think that's how it must be for us—
and maybe, who knows, live happily ever after,
unless the death card really does mean death.

DIDO: You know:
All great love stories end in death,
because the truth of life is that all any of us ever have
is one great love in life,
not two or three or a hundred.
Just one.
And then we die—
whether soon or later, it doesn't matter,
because that's all we are given in life,
only one chance at real love,
and all the rest is just what comes before and after—
and if a love story ended differently
it would be untrue.

Do you cook?

AENEAS: Well, I *like* to cook.

DIDO: What do you like to cook?

AENEAS: I can cook pasta
and fish.

DIDO: Pasta.

AENEAS: I've always thought,
one day,

when I have lots of time
you know,
long afternoons
I'd like to really learn to cook
and make pottery.

DIDO: After we make love.

AENEAS: Right.

When I was a child
I would go for a walk in the woods,
and everyone would say
be careful
stay on the path,
don't wander off the path
or you'll get lost.
And I was always afraid I might wander into the woods
deeper and deeper
and never find my way back again,
and it frightened me until now
when I think of you,
and the voice in the back of my head says
go on
go ahead
go off the path.

[*Dido puts a robe around him*
and moves him to a couch
where there is food and drink.
He lies with his head in her lap.]

DIDO: I was thinking:
we were traveling by camel in the dessert,
and we decided to stop and rest
on a lawn in the suburbs.
My blouse was off.
And there were all these people
playing croquet around us.
We took a walk through the village.

Sometimes we were together
and sometimes apart
and we would meet sometimes.
It was a wonderful community in this village
and we were having a feast at a long table outdoors
and someone gave me a baby
and the baby was you
and everyone was looking at me
and I bent down to kiss you
but I kissed you
as a grownup.

JIM: You know . . .
sometimes I think
I could just put myself in a woman's hands forever
just do exactly what she says.

ALICE: Unh-hunh.

JIM: I like it when a woman climbs on top of me
rests both hands on the bed
looks down at me
and makes love to me, while I
press both hands to her heart.

JOE: Or sits upright on you,
her head thrown back
bringing her feet together
on the bed to one side of your body.

JIM: Yes.

ALICE: Here,
we call that
the Swan.

ANDREA: Or, drawing her feet up close to your side,
a woman might move her hips so that you
circle deep inside her,
we call that the Honey Bee.

ANDREA: Or if she sits astride you,
facing your feet,
and brings both her feet up to your thighs,
and moves her hips
a little, sort of—frantically:
this is known as
the Swan Sport.

ALICE: Or, catching your cock, she
slips it into her quim
clings to you and shakes her buttocks:
this is called the Lovely Lady in Control.

LETTY: And when you hold each other's hands,
sprawled like two starfish making love,
her breasts against your chest,
her thighs stretched out along yours:
this is called the Coitus of the Gods.

CAROL: But when she is tired
and her passion has ebbed,
you should let her rest, bending forward to lay
her forehead on yours
without disturbing your bodies joined together.

LETTY: And sometimes, then
your lover will feel aroused again
and take your penis
in her hand and, shaping
her lips to an O, lay them lightly to its tip,
moving her head in tiny circles.
We call this Touching.

CAROL: And then she lets the head slide
completely
into her mouth
and presses the shaft firmly between her lips,
holding a moment before pulling away.
We call this
Inviting the Nectar.

LETTY: And then taking your penis deep into her mouth,
pulling on it and sucking
as though she were stripping clean a mango-stone:
this is what we call
Sucking a Mango.

JIM: Oh.

JOE: I thought—
for a minute I thought you were a pond
and I slipped into you
you were so cool
and dark

Do you ever dream of the end of the world?
Sometimes
I dream the world is ending,
everything is burning
and there is nowhere to run.

JIM: I haven't really slept much lately myself.
I lie down, but I don't sleep.
I'm always watching the door,
the window,
then back to the door.
I get up five times a night,
to check the windows
sometimes ten or fifteen times.
There's always something within reach,
like a knife or a chair
I used to sleep with a gun underneath my pillow.

[AENEAS *begins to shiver.*]

JOE: If I saw someone down an alley in the dark
I wouldn't go the other way,
I'd go down there thinking,
"Maybe I'll get lucky."
I guess I wanted to be killed.
Once I came on a guy raping a hooker.

She was screaming . . .
and it was easy to tell he was hurting her real bad.
I yelled at him.
And he turned around and started reaching behind his back,
so I knew he was carrying something.
I ran on him so fast and had his elbow before he could pull out his gun
and I pounded the shit out of him.
After that I started carrying a carving fork with me
wherever I went.
I sharpened the tines.
I didn't want to kill anyone.
I figured you could just stick it into somebody so far
before it stopped.

DIDO: Hey!

AENEAS: What?

DIDO: Come here.

What were you thinking?

AENEAS: Oh.
Right now . . .
I was thinking—
well, then I was thinking
I was flying in a small plane
a Piper Cub
a young woman with me
a clear, beautiful day,
so clear in the sky
wonderful sunshine
the fertile landscape below
green fields
streams
small lakes
clear ponds
trees
and I was not only flying
not only exhilirated to be up in the sky

but I was taking off and landing
taking off and landing again and again.
I could go from heaven to earth
and back again
whenever I wanted.

[*She takes him in her arms.*

The CHORUS *steps forward to sing a medley of three love songs.*

As they sing, Dido and Aeneas are together intimately, and a minuscule sailboat crosses from one side of the stage to the other very, very slowly.

Silence.]

AENEAS: Sometimes I worry you will leave me.

DIDO: I leave you?
Never.

AENEAS: Or will you fall in love with someone else?

DIDO: No.

AENEAS: You might.
Make love with someone else.
I think I couldn't bear that.
I knew a man who was married
and had a lover
for thirty years.
He would have dinner with his family
and then go and have dinner with his lover.
Every night for thirty years
he ate two dinners.

DIDO: This is a man you're talking about.
I couldn't make love with anyone but you.

AENEAS: But there are bigamists, you know.

DIDO: These are all men.

[*Silence*]

What I was thinking was:
I was thinking about making love with you
And so I went shopping
and I bought two summer dresses
just simple things
one with lots of tiny buttons down the front
and the other a long tee-shirt dress
sort of suggestive
not the usual sort of thing I wear
and what I was thinking about when I picked them out
was how you would take them off.

AENEAS: Oh.

DIDO: Are you here?

AENEAS: Oh. Sure.

DIDO: Are you worried about yourself?

AENEAS: No.
But I've made promises.

DIDO: Promises?

AENEAS: To go on,
to find a home for those who have come with me.

DIDO: Really.

AENEAS: To take revenge.

It seems remote to me now.

DIDO: So.
You've found a home.

AENEAS: You mean here?

DIDO: Yes.

AENEAS: Well. Or,
you could come with me.

DIDO: Come with you?

AENEAS: Would you?

DIDO: Are you asking me?

AENEAS [*After a moment's pause*]: Yes.

DIDO: My home is here.

AENEAS: You wouldn't leave?

DIDO: Why don't you stay?

AENEAS: This is a woman's world.

DIDO: A woman's world?
What's that?

AENEAS: I don't know, but . . .
it's not a world I've made.
The world I promised I would make.

DIDO: What world was that?

AENEAS: A world
without
false hope
or sentiment.

Ideas we used to have of how things could be
before we learned

in our time
who we really are.

DIDO [*Smiling*]: Is this really what you're saying to me?

AENEAS: Yes.

DIDO: Is this what you really believe?

AENEAS: Yes.

DIDO: Really.

This is your reason you want to leave?

AENEAS: Yes.

[*This is developing into a real, angry lovers' fight.*]

DIDO: Your real reason?

AENEAS: Yes.

DIDO: And you let me fall in love with you?

AENEAS: What?

DIDO: You let me fall in love with you
and you meant to leave?

AENEAS: I didn't mean anything.
I didn't have any intention.
I was lost, remember?
It just happened.

DIDO: Think about it.
Are you awake now?

AENEAS: What?

DIDO: Are you wide awake?

[*As Dido and Aeneas quarrel, the men and women of the chorus turn their backs on one another, walk away from one another, storm offstage, come back mad, push one another, etc.*]

AENEAS: Yes.

DIDO: You loved me when you saw me,
and I loved you.
We fell in love the way people do.
And then take months to find it out
or never do.
But you fell for me right away, didn't you?

[*Long silence*]

AENEAS: Yes.

DIDO: And now you are saying you need to leave
and that the reason is you need to live in a world without hope.
Are you listening to yourself?

[*Silence*]

It's not that you're afraid of me?

AENEAS: Afraid?

DIDO: Afraid it might turn out I really really love you?

AENEAS: Of course not.

DIDO: Or you love me so much you can't help yourself?

[*A moment of his not understanding the question*]

AENEAS: No.

DIDO: You think someone who could love you so much
might be crazy?

AENEAS: No.

DIDO: Not balanced.
Someone who would read Tarot cards
must be crazy?

AENEAS: No.

DIDO: Superstitious.
Kind of fun
but not someone you could feel comfortable with
year in year out.
Someone who might believe in other strange things—
astrological charts
children's stories

AENEAS: No.

DIDO [*Playful*]: the I Ching.

AENEAS: No.

DIDO: You wouldn't lie to me?

[*Silence*]

Because I'm blond?

AENEAS: Because you're blond?

DIDO: Because I'm foreign to you?

AENEAS: No.

DIDO: Because I'm a woman?

AENEAS: What?

DIDO [*She speaks not with anger but with considerateness—as though she might help him past his fears if she can discover them*]:
So different.
Such another world.
Such a foreign country
to settle down in and feel at home.
So unfamiliar.
Such a different landscape,
such a different way of looking out and seeing the world around you.
You might become a different person altogether
living here,
a kind of person you wouldn't even recognize.
Are you afraid you might not be able to tell where it all might end.
What our lives might become.
How we might become lost in one another.

[AENEAS *exits.*]

Or else, that you will give up the life you know
and then find out this life of ours collapses, too,
and you'll be lost,
it will be too late to recover what you had,
you'll end your life alone
in some country you never meant to come to,
no shape left to your life,
no point, no goal, no aim.

It could end—
this love at first glance—
it could just be infatuation

[AENEAS *returns.*]

a fling
no lasting love
or it could lead to something so deep
so lifelong,
such a commitment

to another person
who might die
or make a life with you
no one can control,
and you don't know me,
stepping into the unknown
your only life.
For all eternity
this would be your fate.

[*Silence*]

Stay for a while.
See if time
will change things for you.

[*Dido makes her way to the hot tub and climbs in.*]

AENEAS: If I stay I'm afraid I'll never leave.
But I'll stay from weakness,
from failure to keep my word,
not from strength.

[*During the following speech, the men of the chorus, lined up against the back
wall, say everything Aeneas says, before he says it, overlapping with Aeneas in
frantic explanation, so that* all *the men are expressing these thoughts.*]

You know,
I have to think about my age
and my health,
how long I have to do the things I set out to do in the world
in order to feel okay about myself,
do the things I think I am capable of doing
even have some talent, or gift
even what I *like* to do,
I mean what I've been trained to do.
I don't know if this is a difference between men and women
where men can't
in a way
just follow their hearts

but have to honor certain obligations they have made
and things to do *in the world*
as men/people who were meant to achieve something.
Plus I have *obligations.*

I mean
I have a friend who had a career
in Haiti and South Africa and Paris
doing what he thought he could.
This was someone who had been a conscientious objector.
Or another friend who has been a prison doctor,
a prison doctor all these years,
you know what a thankless task that is.
This guy is a saint,
and I think, What am I doing?
There are certain things—
the goals a man has for his life:
politics
his career
to feel good about himself
to feel he is someone,
or even just to honor the commitments he has made,
to feel he is an honest person
a man
who can be counted on.
What else is it to be a man
if, when you give your word,
it can be counted on,
you stand for something
which is, I mean, whether you believe in immortality or not,
what you have to contribute
the best you can do
having been raised to *do* something.
men are meant to *do* something
or else they've just never existed,
stand by something
be ready to die for it
put their lives on the line.
There may even be some deep biological thing to this.

[Aeneas speaks by himself.]

I feel it.
I feel I can't let it go
without just
annihilating myself.

[Silence]

DIDO: Okay.
Then go.

AENEAS: What?

DIDO: Go ahead.
Go.
If that's what you need to do,
I understand.

AENEAS: Thank you.

[Silence.

*They hug for a moment
and then Dido grabs Aeneas by the hair
and pushes him under water.
The movements among the men and women become violent,
as they push and slam each other into the wall
and throw one another to the ground.*

*Dido picks up Aeneas's head—he comes up gasping—
and pushes it under the water again and again.*

*They are thrashing wildly.
She is plunging his head under water over and over.
Finally she leaves him submerged.*

*She drags herself out of the hot tub,
exhausted,
lies on the floor.*

The CHORUS *sings a couple of stanzas of "When Somebody Loves You."*

While the chorus sings this final song, Aeneas drags himself from the hot tub. He is nearly dead—or else, he doesn't drag himself from the tub, and he is dead.

AENEAS *collapses on the floor.*

The CHORUS *members are variously finding their way back to one another, embracing one another.*

Slowly, Aeneas drags himself across the floor and puts his arm around Dido, who lies face down on the floor. They lie together, both on their stomachs, exhausted, his arm around her facing opposite directions.]

CHORUS: But if you'll let me love you
it's for sure I'm gonna love you
all the way.

[*Lights out.*]

THE END

Time to Burn

Time to Burn, inspired by Maxim Gorky's *Lower Depths*, was first produced at Steppenwolf Theatre in Chicago, where it was directed by Tina Landau.

Time to Burn

Characters

JESSIE	TERTIUS
BILLY	ANNA
JAROSLAW	NIKOS
RAUL	NGUYEN
KADIRA	SHLOMO
VINNIE PAZZI	TRANG
ALEJANDRO	POLICEMAN

Nighttime.

America.

The sound of water dripping into buckets here and there.

We are moving very slowly in darkness
through a vast, dead, peeling, rusting, leaking,
disintegrating factory building.

In the darkness we can barely make out huge, useless, abandoned nineteenth-
    century machines—big incomprehensible things
no longer capable of giving employment to anyone.

Lightbulbs—not now lit—inside conical green glass shades,
hang down from wires that go up three stories to the ceiling,
where there are just a half-dozen small windows.

In the center of this vast room are two rows of cutting tables—
steel frame tables with wooden work surfaces worn smooth—
on which workers once produced things.

Now we see, as we move very slowly through the darkness,
that a dozen or so people are sleeping on these tables.

As we move along the aisles separating the two rows of tables,
we see things on the floor next to the tables—
a neatly placed pair of terribly worn boots,
a stack of beautiful, leather-bound books,
a pile of junk from the streets.

As we continue to move, we see,
in white type dropped out of the darkness, the title: Time to Burn.

We hear a door opening
and look up to see,
on a landing
at the top of a double flight of stairs at one end of the factory,
a man, quietly, carefully close a door behind himself,
wait a moment,
and then come down the stairs.

The dawn light is beginning to come through the windows
high up in the wall.

The man, BILLY,
makes his way noiselessly through the room,
past the sleeping people
to a cluster of four wooden wine crates, makeshift shelves,
near an empty sleeping space.

He takes out of his pockets, and puts into these shelves,
some small tools,
a cluster of keys,
and a handful of jewelry.

We hear nothing, but,
with Billy, we turn to look
and see an elderly black woman, JESSIE,
who is awake and looking with intent curiosity at Billy.

JESSIE: What have you got?

BILLY: Nothing.

JESSIE: I see you've got something.
What is it?
I've got jewelry, you know, if that's what you want.

[*She starts to rummage through the bags of stuff around her.*]

A watch
you know,
or a tortoiseshell comb,
barometer.
You see it?
A barometer,
a precious old thing.

[*We see that one of the other sleepers,
a young woman just next to Jessie named Kadira,
has awakened
and turned only her head to look at Jessie,
sleepily,
without saying anything, as Jessie goes on.*]

BILLY [*Agreeably*]: Where did you get that?

JESSIE [*With indifference*]: I found it.
[*Then, interested again*]
An almanac
sea shells
a tweezer case
eyebrow brush

Here they are:
a pair of silk garters.
You like these?

JAROSLAW: Ssshhhh!!! Quiet.

BILLY [*Whispering*]: No, thank you.

[*Silence*]

JESSIE: I have a snuff box.

BILLY: Unh-hunh.

JESSIE: Do you like snuff?

BILLY: Snuff?
I don't use snuff.

JESSIE: Don't use snuff.

BILLY: No.
Where did you get this stuff?

JAROSLAW: Will you be quiet!

[*Silence*]

JESSIE: I thought gentlemen used snuff.

BILLY [*Still agreeable, friendly toward Jessie*]:
Well, it may have been true of gentlemen in the twenties
or something,
I don't know,
but I've never used it.

JESSIE: Well, I have a bell pull . . .
[*She holds it up.*]

BILLY: Oh, well, that's handy.

JESSIE: I have a bell to go with it.
Somewhere here.
[*She rummages around, somewhat lost in it all;
she comes upon her bottle, takes a moment to have a drink.*]
Curling irons
[*Looking up*]
for the hair you know . . .

BILLY: Yes.

[JESSIE *shakes her head, a little bit put out with how many keys she has.
Jessie is lost in a world of objects, of commodities, yes—
each one precious to her—
but more than that, lost in objects of the past, of a former life,
of history.
She holds one up.*]

BILLY: Very handsome.

JESSIE: cork screws, of course
bits of brass.
That's from another time.

[*Our gaze travels to Jaroslaw just as he starts to speak.*]

JAROSLAW: Do you know there are people here who are still trying to sleep!

JESSIE: Then you have your usual utensils
pans
a stuffed bird
[*This stops her; she gazes at it for a while before plumping it back down
unceremoniously.*]
opera glasses—very hard to find—you wouldn't think it—people don't throw
    them away—I don't know what they do with them
[*To Billy*]
but, well, this is the stuff of life on earth.

BILLY: Is it?

JESSIE: One time I had a desk
that had belonged to my mother and father
and before that to my mother's mother,
and after they were gone
I could put my hand out flat in the center of the desk
where my father's hand had been
and feel that close to him.
And now the desk is gone, too.

JAROSLAW: Inconsiderate bastards . . .

[*Silence*]

JESSIE: Well, would you like a snuff box anyway?

BILLY: I don't think so, thank you.

Look—
now—
these are beautiful things,
but I don't have any place to keep them.

JESSIE: Oh.
[*Offended*]
Oh, of course.
[*With sudden distaste*]
These things are not in fashion.

BILLY: No, that's not . . .

JESSIE: They're just trash, you know.

BILLY: No, no, I didn't mean . . .

JESSIE [*Not mollified*]: Think nothing of it.

JAROSLAW: What is it about you people?
You think you're the only people in the world?
You don't give a damn if other people are trying to get some rest?

[*We look around the factory.*
Others are just waking up now,
or trying not to wake up,
pulling on their clothes.

One sits for a long while on the edge of the table, his head down,
collecting himself;
another holds his head in his hands,
JESSIE *moves on to wrapping her swollen ankles tightly with ace bandages,*

A man is scratching himself,
another man is putting ear drops into his ear.

With all the disabilities and ailments,
this looks like a wounded army camped here.

ANNA, *still in bed, coughs*
deeply and for a long while.]

BILLY [*To Jaroslaw*]: She needs a doctor.

JAROSLAW: She needs a blanket.

BILLY: You should take her to a doctor.

JAROSLAW: Mind your own business.
She's my wife.

[*The door bangs open.*
On the landing is RAUL
struggling to get something through the door.
His cursing is heavily accented—
a foreigner who learned all the swear words first.
He is Mexican—and has several disabilities:
an odd manner that suggests a neurological deficit of some sort;
and he might also be a dwarf,
or have one leg much shorter than the other.]

RAUL: God damn this fucking son of a bitch, you fucking cocksucker.

BILLY: You need help?

RAUL: What do you think?
This fucking cocksucker
goddammit.

[BILLY *starts for the stairs.*
When RAUL *pulls the thing suddenly through the door,*
it hits the landing rail
and pieces of it fly over the rail down into the factory.]

RAUL: Hey, you fuck . . .

JAROSLAW: Look out!

KADIRA [*Frightened*]: Hey! Fuck! Fuck!

[*The people below scatter.*]

JAROSLAW: People are still sleeping here goddammit!

RAUL: Goddam you cocksucker!

[RAUL *kicks the thing,*
tears pieces off it and throws them over the rail
and kicks the remainder of it down the stairs.]

There, you son of a bitch
you goddam fucker,
you fuck with me
I'll tear your fucking lungs out.

[*Silence*]

BILLY: What is this?

RAUL: It's a barbecue.
I found it on the street.
I thought we could cook dinner.

JESSIE: Cook dinner?

RAUL: Have a party.

[*Everyone comes forward now with interest to examine the pieces.*]

KADIRA [*Yelling at Raul*]: Then why the fuck did you ruin it?

RAUL [*Yelling*]: I didn't fucking ruin it.
The fucking thing wouldn't fit through the fucking door.

KADIRA [*Yelling*]: It fits through the door if you'd use your fucking head.

RAUL [*Yelling*]: You're so fucking smart.
You use your fucking head then and put it back together.

[*Silence*]

BILLY: We can put it back together.

[*He begins to pick up the pieces,
others come to help him.*

*At the top of a second set of stairs,
at the end of the factory opposite to
the stairs we have seen used till now,
VINNIE PAZZI, the landlord, suddenly appears.
He wears yellow rubber gloves (at all times),
polyester satin alligator-patterned trousers,
and a black, see-through polyamide tank top,
and sunglasses.*]

VINNIE PAZZI [*Angrily*]: What's this goddam noise?

[*Silence*]

ALEJANDRO: Raul dropped something.

VINNIE PAZZI: Did he?
Or did you think you'd wreck the place?

[*He starts down the stairs, talking all the way.*]

You think it can't get worse?
You think I can't get other tenants who would appreciate a warm place to
   sleep?
You people.
A few bucks a month and you think you're being gouged.
I could have a waiting list if I wanted to.
And what's this all over the floor?
Didn't you people sweep this morning?

You think the rats and cockroaches won't come around
no matter what sort of filth you live in?
Spreading their diseases right up the stairs into my home?
What is this?

RAUL: A barbecue.

VINNIE PAZZI: A what?

RAUL: A barbecue.

JESSIE: For a party.

VINNIE PAZZI: You mean you think you'll have a fire down here?

BILLY: It's all contained—
just charcoal, you know,
for cooking dinner.

VINNIE PAZZI: What is the matter with you people?
You won't be happy till you burn my house down?
Do you think the fire department would allow you to
cook down here?
Here's your problem in a nutshell.
You can't think.
No wonder.
Your minds don't let you conceive more than one step ahead.
Now pick this junk up and get it out of here.

BILLY: Wait a minute.

[*Silence*]

The barbecue stays.

[*Silence*]

VINNIE PAZZI: And who do you think you are?

BILLY: I am the guy who gave you a Rolex watch with an alligator band five days ago and you owe me my share of what you sold it for. That's who I am. Who do you think you are?

[*Silence.*

Vinnie Pazzi looks around at all the witnesses.]

VINNIE PAZZI: This is no conversation to have in front of all these people.

BILLY: I didn't start it.

VINNIE PAZZI: Come upstairs.

BILLY: I'm busy here, as you can see.

VINNIE PAZZI: I see.

[*Silence*]

All right then.
We'll settle our business later.

BILLY: Meanwhile, the barbecue stays.

VINNIE PAZZI: Oh,
it does.

BILLY: Yes.

VINNIE PAZZI: Unh-hunh.

BILLY: So long as you do whatever you want
we will do whatever we want.

VINNIE PAZZI: I see.

BILLY: And you need to learn to speak to us
with some respect.

VINNIE PAZZI: I see.

[*Silence.*

Vinnie Pazzi looks around.]

And you, Mister Kacewicz,
I speak to you with all respect,
what is this around your bunk?

JAROSLAW: What?

VINNIE PAZZI: All this shit.

JAROSLAW: All this is my work.
I manufacture computer components.

VINNIE PAZZI: Here?
On my premises?

JAROSLAW: Well, yes.
It's like a—home factory.
I put my faith in capitalism, you know.
This is the new age,
the information age.
People can work from their own homes.

VINNIE PAZZI: Oh, good.
If you're taking up such space for a commercial enterprise,
I guess I'll have to raise your rent.
Say another ten dollars a month.

JAROSLAW: Ten dollars a month?

VINNIE PAZZI: Or twenty.

JAROSLAW: Twenty dollars a month?

VINNIE PAZZI: It's not enough?

JAROSLAW: Why don't you just shoot me?

VINNIE PAZZI: Shoot you,
you dumb fuck,
what good would that do me?

BILLY [*Speaking confidentially*]:
You know, he doesn't make any money at it.

VINNIE PAZZI: Well, that's none of my business, is it?
How well you do, what profit comes your way,
that's up to you, isn't it?
Work all you want.
I wish you well.
As they say:
a rising tide lifts all boats, eh?
But I'll have to have my commercial rent, won't I?
And I don't buy luxuries either, any more than you do.
I'll use it to buy a statue of St. Jude.
You'll share the credit for it.

JAROSLAW: Credit?

VINNIE PAZZI: Credit in the next world, my friend.
Every deed,
every word
every sacrifice
is entered into a man's account there.

You shouldn't abandon your religion, you know.
That's what's wrong these days.

In the next world,
we'll all be equal.

That's heaven, you know.

[*He continues speaking very quietly.*]

But, meanwhile, here on earth,
there is the matter of sweeping up.
This is, in a certain sense, beyond my control.
I have the health department to answer to, haven't I?

[*He turns to go back upstairs,
turns back.*]

Do you understand?
They shut places down
for violations.
Throw everyone out and shut them down.
Do I make myself perfectly clear?

[*They watch in silence
as he goes up the stairs and out.*]

JAROSLAW: Where am I going to get twenty dollars a month?
You prick.

BILLY: Don't worry,
we'll all chip in.

JAROSLAW: How do you mean chip in?

BILLY: Chip in.
No reason you should pay the whole barbecue tax yourself.

RAUL: Really, there are no better people in the world than thieves.

JAROSLAW: Sure. Money comes easy to them—they don't have to work.

JESSIE: Money comes easy to plenty of people,
but it doesn't come so easy to let it go.

ALEJANDRO: As for work, now,
if you make it pleasant for me,
I'll be delighted to work.

JAROSLAW: Make it pleasant for you.
Right.
That's all you people want is to have something handed to you.

ALEJANDRO [*Drily*]: No doubt it's cultural.

RAUL [*Continuing the mockery*]: Cultural, yes.
Or genetic.

JAROSLAW: Yes, let's be honest.
You're used to living on the dole,
you Third World people.
Well, it's a different world now, you know.
You'll have to pull your own weight now, you know.

RAUL: I think my people have pulled their weight.

JAROSLAW: You do? I don't see it, anywhere I go.
People looking for a handout.
I've worked for everything I ever got in life
and what will become of me?
I own nothing.

RAUL: Well, the point is you had a job all these years!
I haven't even got a job!

JAROSLAW: Who asked you to come here?
Go home.
Go home.

KADIRA: You go home!
Where do you think you are?

ALEJANDRO: Joy
makes you open and light.
Joy
counteracts the pull of gravity.
Joy
banishes the consciousness of self.

Joy is more than contentment,
more than happiness.
Joy has something of the sacred in it,
something we should all have every day.

[*Silence*]

[*A door opens
at the top of the double stairway that Billy descended earlier.
Tertius steps out onto the landing and stands motionlessly there.*

*A vision of Boston Brahmin elegance and grace,
fine clothes and manners,
enters this world of filth and rags like a dream.
The inhabitants of the factory all turn one by one
and look up at Tertius in silence, and even awe.
He descends the stairs slowly,
unable to shed a bearing of natural dignity—
and slight physical awkwardness, as though he were not quite accustomed to
     having to walk about the earth on foot—
and with a certain care of his self, as though he might be breakable,
as though his pockets were filled with uncooked eggs—
and they remain silent all the while he descends the stairs.*]

TERTIUS: Good morning.

BILLY: Good morning.

TERTIUS: I was told one of you might direct me to my accommodations.

ALEJANDRO: Your accommodations?

BILLY [*Amicably*]: A place to sleep?

TERTIUS: Yes. Indeed.

BILLY [*Gesturing*]: Over here there's room . . .

TERTIUS: Thank you.

[*He moves through the crowd:*
Billy, an amiable midwesterner
Raul, from Mexico
Kadira, a young Eastern European woman
Jessie, an elderly African American woman
Jaroslaw and his wife, both Poles
Alejandro, a Brazilian transvestite]

Tertius Hodgson.
Pleased to make your acquaintance.

BILLY: Billy.

[*Tertius greets each one with "How do you do?"*]

ALEJANDRO: Alejandro.

JAROSLAW: Jaroslaw Kacewicz
My wife, Anna.

KADIRA: Kadira.

BILLY [*As Tertius stops before an empty space on a table*]: We're not as—
handsomely equipped as you might be used to.

TERTIUS: Thank you.
This looks quite comfortable to me.

JESSIE: You're a gentleman.
Well, I should say, probably, an aristocrat.

[*Tertius shrugs amiably.*]

JESSIE [*To the others*]: You know, as they say,
aristocracy is like the smallpox.
A man may get well, but the pock marks remain.

[*Silence; she recognizes her faux pas.*]

Actually, what I meant to say . . .

TERTIUS [*Waving it off with complete good humor and equanimity*]:
No, no, no. I think you're probably quite right.
Pock marks indeed.

BILLY: What brings you here?

TERTIUS: Well, a love of cards, I should say,
primarily.
A love of anything that moves really—
on which a man may place a bet and lose large sums of money—
the stock market, pork bellies, horses

BILLY: The sport of kings.
You know—because if you believe in horse racing
then you believe that ancestry counts.

RAUL: Proving once again: the main thing is luck.

BILLY: Luck?
Breeding I'd have said.

TERTIUS: Well.
Nurture maybe.

ALEJANDRO: I don't think anyone believes in that any more.

JESSIE: Hard work.
Character.

[*Shocked silence,
then laughter from all sides.
The laughter goes on and on and on.
They laugh until they cry.*]

[ANNA, *coming out of the laughter, coughs horribly
and for a long, long time
while they all look at her, waiting for her to stop;
awkward silence.*]

BILLY: We were going to have breakfast.
Will you join us?

TERTIUS: Thank you.

[*Billy pours a cup of coffee for Tertius.*
Others gather around the coffee pot, pour cups of coffee,
and break off pieces of stale bread from a couple of loaves.]

JESSIE: Of course, this is not a typical day for us.
Normally we wake up quite late in the morning
stretch out a hand to reach for some chocolate,
which we eat, customarily, lying in bed;
and then we get up for breakfast at eight
when we have porridge,
plum cake,
eggs benedict,
a little halibut or
some other fish,
hot biscuits and butter,
with raspberry jam and
café au lait.

[*We look around the room slowly,*
going from face to face as she gives this loving recital.]

And then,
really,
our day begins.

TERTIUS: I should feel quite at home.

JESSIE: And just recently we have acquired a barbecue.

RAUL: We thought we might have a party.

ALEJANDRO: A garden party.

TERTIUS: A garden party.

BILLY: So.
Alejandro, would you help me sweep up?

ALEJANDRO: It's not my turn to sweep today.
It's Jaroslaw's turn.

JAROSLAW: I've no time to clean up,
I have work to do.

ALEJANDRO: That's not my business.
It's your turn to sweep.
I'm not going to do other people's work.

JAROSLAW: This is your problem,
you won't lift a finger,
let the whole world sink into rot.
I *am* working.

ALEJANDRO: Who is he talking to?

JAROSLAW: I'm talking to you, you slut.

ALEJANDRO: Who are you calling a slut, you asshole?

TERTIUS: Never mind.
I'll help.
It will be a novelty for me, you know.

RAUL: Although, let's face it,
you are a slut.
[*To the others*]
I mean, I don't approve of his behavior either.

KADIRA: Oh, no, you'd fuck him up the ass,
you just wouldn't approve of his behavior.

RAUL: Fuck him?
You think I fuck men?

ALEJANDRO: You know, there are certain things a man knows.
For instance:
have you heard of Inviting the Nectar?

RAUL: Inviting the Nectar?

ALEJANDRO: When a man lets another man's penis
slide completely into his mouth

JAROSLAW: This is disgusting.

ALEJANDRO: and presses the shaft firmly between his lips,
holding a moment before pulling away
this is called
Inviting the Nectar.

JAROSLAW: This is what's wrong if you ask me.

ALEJANDRO: Or a man can take your penis deep into his mouth,
pulling on it and sucking
as though he were stripping clean a mango-stone:
this is what we call
Sucking a Mango.

JAROSLAW: Sick.

ALEJANDRO: You shouldn't be listening to this.

JAROSLAW: You talk here in front of everyone.

ALEJANDRO: Where should I go to talk? Don't I live here?

KADIRA: Come with me shopping.
We'll get things for the picnic.

RAUL: Why do you think I fuck men?

TERTIUS: While you're out, you might pick up some champagne.

KADIRA: So you don't fuck men.

ALEJANDRO [*To Raul*]: Sometimes, you know,
before you make love
you can massage your penis
with honey mixed with powdered black pepper,
and you'll find you can go on and on.
Women like this.

[RAUL *looks at him uncomprehendingly.*]

Just a suggestion.

TERTIUS: I say,
while you're out,
you might pick up some champagne.

RAUL: Sure.
What do you like?

TERTIUS: Whatever is closest to the door.

RAUL: Right.
Sure.

[*Raul leaves with Kadira.*
Billy and Tertius sweep.
Nikos emerges from the shadows
and approaches Tertius, talking to him, in Greek.
(The English translation is not delivered; it's given here just for the actors' conve-
nience.)]

NIKOS: Leepon, eenu chris mos apop sila-stall menos y anna cani ola ta pragh
mata ee bua hoha.
[So it is the oracle from high, sent to make all things amenable.]

TERTIUS: Ah.
Aeschylus.

NIKOS: Kalo-so-ree-sa-te. To on-o-ma mou ee-ne Nikos.
[Welcome, my name is Nikos.]

TERTIUS: Ah.
[*Turning to Nikos*]
He-ro-me poe-lee.
See-gno-mee
alla te elee-nee-ka-mou
then ee-ne ke to-so k-la e(x)ho na ta mee-lee-so ar-ke-to ke-ro.
[I'm glad to meet you.
Forgive me, but my Greek is a little rusty.
I haven't spoken it in a while.]

[*They shake hands.*]

BILLY: You speak Greek?

TERTIUS: Yes, I suppose I do.

NIKOS: See-gno-mee e an ee-me lee-go af-thor-mee-tos,
alla ee-me ka-lo-tech-nees, ee-tho-pee-os ya teen ak-ree-veea,
ke e-(x)hi pe-ra-see lee-gos ke-ros.
[Excuse me if I seem a bit forward,
but I'm an artist, an actor really,
and it has been quite some time.]

BILLY: What does he say?

TERTIUS: He is an actor.
Between engagements.

BILLY: Yes.
Well,
of course he's between engagements.

I mean: he speaks Greek.

NIKOS: Lexo pros humas tond Athenaias megan
thesman delcayos mandi-son duf sef-soni.

[I will speak justly before you, Athena's great tribunal—
since I am a prophet, I cannot lie.

TERTIUS [*Applauding*]: Bravo.
Bravo.
[*To Billy*]
The Eumenides.
One of my favorite plays in fact.
[*To Nikos*]
To men dikaion touth hoson sthenei mathein
[Learn how strong this plea of justice is;
and I tell you to obey the will of my father,]

NIKOS [*Once again, with great truth and power as an actor*]:
boulei piphausko d umm epispesthai patros:
horkos gar outi Zenos ischuei pleon.
for an oath is not more powerful.]

TERTIUS: Zeus, hos legeis su, tonde chresmon opase.
[Zeus, as you say, gave you this oracular command.]

BILLY: You know it, too.

TERTIUS: Well, a few lines.
He knows the whole thing.
He's performed it a dozen times, he says.

BILLY [*Looking at Nikos with a new respect*]:
Really.
A dozen times.

[BILLY *and* NIKOS *exchange silent acknowledgement.*
Nikos turns away,
goes to his bunk.
TERTIUS *and Billy sweep.*]

BILLY: I often thought I should have been an actor.

TERTIUS: Unh-hunh.

BILLY: But then, it's no way to make a living.

TERTIUS: No.

BILLY: You must have some money left, though.

TERTIUS: How do you mean?

BILLY: It's hard to believe you don't have *any* money left.

TERTIUS [*Good naturedly*]: It's hard for *me* to believe.

BILLY: But probably you still have some connections.
I mean, if you had an idea for a business.
You know, I have some ideas for businesses.

TERTIUS: Really? What sort of businesses?

BILLY: Well, it would depend on what sort of resources someone had to bring
to it, you know.

TERTIUS: Really, I'm afraid I burned all my bridges.

BILLY: Really.
No one, you know, we might have lunch with.

TERTIUS [*Smiling*]: No, I'm afraid not.

BILLY: Well.
No hard feelings that I . . .

TERTIUS: No. No.
Certainly not.
Certainly not.

[*This is a long, long quiet time.*
We watch JAROSLAW *work at his computer parts.*
He is trying to force a small piece into another.
He grows angrier and angrier,
and finally explodes in anger.]

JAROSLAW: Da mu eba maikata! Pochti uspyah.
[Fuck. Fuck. I almost got it.]
Izvinyavai. Molya te, Anna, prosti mi.
[I'm sorry. Please forgive me, Anna.]

ANNA: Zanam, zanam.
[I know, I know.]

JAROSLAW: Opitvam se da izkaram pari, da te premestya v bolnitsa.
[I'm trying to make some money to put you in a hospital.]

ANNA: Ne iskam da umra v bolnitsa.
[I don't want to die in a hospital.]

JAROSLAW: Koi govori za umirane be chovek . . .
[Who's talking about dying . . .]

ANNA: Ostavi me na mira.
[Leave me.]

JAROSLAW: Zashto mislish nai-loshoto?
[Why do you think the worst?]

ANNA: Taka e po-dobre!
[It's better that way!]

[*He shakes his head from side to side
finally letting it fall to his chest
probably in tears.*

*We look at Anna.
She goes on coughing.
Finally subsides, exhausted,
closes her eyes.*]

JESSIE: Of all human qualities, the greatest is sympathy.

ALESSANDRA: Or compassion.

JESSIE: Or compassion.
Sometimes I think:
There are things on my horizon that go beyond me.
There are feelings that rise and rush over me
as if they were written on the walls of my soul-chamber
in some unknown language.
And I am helpless before them.

[*Again: a long, long quiet time.*
Our gaze moves along
to Billy who is taking a radio from a cardboard box.
He plugs it in, turns it on.

Gershwin.
Everyone listens.
A beautiful love song
from another world.

Billy looks away from the radio, listening.
Our gaze moves along
to Nikos, who is preparing heroin to inject.
We watch him do it.
He lies back and listens to Gershwin.

Our gaze moves along
to Jessie, rummaging in her shopping cart full of junk.
She is drinking out of a bottle.
One of her feet is thickly bandaged,
so that she cannot wear a shoe on it.

Our gaze moves along
to Kadira, who is absently shooting craps by herself
and listening to Gershwin.
She begins to sing along quietly, mumblingly, with the radio.

After a moment or two, Alejandro joins in more overtly.
After another moment, Jessie joins in.
Then Billy.

Finally they are all singing this beautiful sentimental song
with great feeling,
each of them caught up in a private world of memory and longing.

After the song, there is a long silence, and then:
The door to the landlord's house opens.

NGUYEN, *a Thai woman, enters with the old man* SHLOMO,
giving him some support as they start down the stairs.
Nguyen speaks with a pronounced Thai accent.]

NGUYEN: Will someone give me a hand?

BILLY: I will.

[*He goes quickly up the stairs to help with Shlomo.*]

NGUYEN: This is a new guy.

BILLY: Hello.
My name is Billy.

SHLOMO: How do you do?
I'm Shlomo.
Really I can manage alone.

BILLY: Of course.
But these are difficult stairs.

SHLOMO: Well, you're an honest man.

BILLY: I'm sorry?

SHLOMO: I say, you are an honest man.

[*Billy and Nguyen exchange a look.*]

BILLY: Ah. Yes.
About the stairs.

SHLOMO: And if you are dishonest about everything else,
what do I care?
You jump up to help an old man.
You're a good human being.

BILLY [*Another look to Nguyen*]: Thank you.
It's kind of you to say so.

[*They are down the stairs now.*]

SHLOMO: Where shall I settle down?

BILLY: Just over here.

[*Shlomo has a tea kettle on a rope over his shoulder and a backpack. Billy takes Shlomo's backpack from him.*]

Here, let me help.

[*Billy puts the backpack on the old man's bunk.*]

I see you've brought your own tea kettle.
Would you like a cup of tea?

SHLOMO: Yes, I would, thank you.

BILLY [*Taking the kettle from the pack*]: I'll do it.

JAROSLAW: What a fascinating old man you've brought to us, Nguyen.
I wonder where he's from.

NGUYEN [*Gently, not harshly*]: You should save all your fascination for your
wife, Jaroslaw.
She needs you.

JAROSLAW: Everyone lectures me.

NGUYEN: You ought to treat her more kindly.
It won't be long now—

JAROSLAW: Don't I know?

NGUYEN [*Still gently*]: It's not enough to know.
You need to understand.
It's a frightening thing to die.

JAROSLAW [*To the others*]: Here I have a child telling me about death.
And meanwhile what about life?

NGUYEN: What am I doing here?
I should get a job as a waitress.

JAROSLAW: You couldn't get a job in a Chinese noodle shop.

NGUYEN [*To Billy*]: He still thinks I'm Chinese.

JAROSLAW: You should get out in the world.
What do you know about anything?
You have such a sheltered life.
You come here with your sister,
she marries this rich man,

BILLY: Rich!

JAROSLAW: a man of property!
More than I have!
I pay him the rent,
he just sits around
lets these Orientals do his work for him.
[*To Nguyen again*]
You're a kept woman really,
what's the difference.

BILLY: I thought you owned the place.

NGUYEN: My sister and I.

BILLY: Your sister and you.
So really the landlord,
he's a kept man.

JAROSLAW: How do you end up owning this place?
Who did you fuck to do that?

BILLY: Jesus.

[*A moment of silence.* RAUL *and* KADIRA *return with arms full of groceries.*]

NGUYEN: No problem.
I'll be out of here pretty soon.

BILLY: Oh?

NGUYEN: I've had enough.
I'll be gone before much longer.

BILLY: When are you leaving?

NGUYEN: I don't know.

[*Silence*]

But the big idea:
getting out of here—
I'm clear on that.

BILLY: Oh, I'm clear on that, too.

NGUYEN: You're going?

BILLY: Sure.

NGUYEN: When?

BILLY: I thought I'd go with you.

[*She looks taken aback.*]

BILLY: It takes courage just to pick up and go.

SHLOMO: Does it?

BILLY: You don't think it does?

SHLOMO: I wouldn't know.
I've done it so many times, ich fargessen.
I don't remember.

KADIRA: You get to know the lay of the land some place,
you think:
better not go somewhere you know nothing.

RAUL: Unless there's no hope at all
then you have to take your chances.

RAUL: Right.

ALEJANDRO: Be a risk taker.

RAUL: Right.

ALEJANDRO: Lead the way.

RAUL: Right.

ALEJANDRO: I sometimes think: this is what I'm doing:
showing the world which way it's going.
This is how it will be for everyone in another ten years.

NGUYEN: It's not so easy for me.
They have my papers.
They say if I leave
they'll have me arrested.

SHLOMO: Your brother-in-law has your papers?

NGUYEN: Yes.

SHLOMO: Why?

NGUYEN: That's how he keeps me here.

[*She turns and goes.*
They all watch her.

SHLOMO *sings,*
maybe something like "When Somebody Loves You."]

BILLY: What's that?

SHLOMO: I'm singing.

[*Continues singing.*]

BILLY: Well, you can stop now.

SHLOMO: You don't like singing?

BILLY: I like it when it's good.

SHLOMO: I don't sing well?

BILLY: No.

SHLOMO: Imagine that! And I thought I did.
It's always like that.
A man thinks to himself: I'm doing a good job.
Then, bang—everyone is displeased.

BILLY: You sing fine.
I just need fresh air.

[*He turns and goes up the stairs to the outdoors.*]

SHLOMO: People's feelings are so mysterious, are they not?
Now here is a woman
[*Gesturing to Alejandro*]
reading a book
and crying.
Not real life!
A book!

RAUL [*Handing Shlomo a cup of tea*]: She's not a woman.

SHLOMO: This young woman?

RAUL: No, she's a transvestite.

SHLOMO: Oh.
Well, then,
a transvestite reading a book—
and crying!
These human beings are strange creatures.

[TRANG, *another Thai woman, appears at the top of the stairs.*
She wears a very expensive, brightly flowered silk robe.
Her hair is done up in a wild top knot with a silk scarf.
When she enters, SHLOMO goes about keeping a low profile by taking out a
project of his own and working on it—hand-binding a book.]

TRANG [*Coming down the stairs*]: Raul, you bastard,
who do you think you are
saying whatever you please about me?

RAUL: What?
I said nothing about you.

TRANG: People tell me what you say.
You know, you can be evicted.
If I told my husband what you say
he'd have you out of here in an instant.
[*To Alejandro*]
Why do you let him talk like this?

ALEJANDRO: Who am I, his keeper?

TRANG: I don't care who you are,
you're living here on charity, remember that.
How much do you owe me?

ALEJANDRO: Who's counting?

RAUL: What did I say?

TRANG: You know what you said.
These rumors about me and Billy.

RAUL: These are not rumors.

TRANG: And if you keep talking like that, you'll be out of here.

[*To Shlomo*]

Who are you? Who are you?

SHLOMO: Just an old man passing through. Don't touch.

TRANG: Who brought you in here?

ALEJANDRO: Your sister.

TRANG: Oh, she did.
No one told me.
How long do you plan to stay?

SHLOMO: That depends.

TRANG: On what?

SHLOMO: On how welcome I am.

RAUL: He's gone out.

TRANG: Who?

RAUL: Billy.

TRANG: Did I ask?

RAUL: I see you looking everywhere.

TRANG: I'm looking to see that everything is in order,
and why hasn't the floor been swept?
How many times have I told you the floor must be swept?

ALEJANDRO: We just swept it.

TRANG: How could I tell?

ALEJANDRO: Well, if you'd been here before it was swept
you could tell.
I can tell.

TRANG: Was my sister just here?

ALEJANDRO: She just brought in the old man.

RAUL: Billy went out.
He went out alone.

TRANG: Did I ask?

[*She turns, goes back up the stairs.*
They watch her go.
ANNA *has a paroxysm of coughing.*
SHLOMO *puts aside his bookbinding.*]

SHLOMO: Here.
Have some tea with me.

ANNA: What good will that do?

SHLOMO: It won't do any good,
but I think you'll like it. It can't hurt.
What's your name?

ANNA: Anna.

SHLOMO: Anna. A beautiful name. My name is Shlomo.

ANNA: As I look at you, you remind me of my father,
just as kind, and soft.

SHLOMO [*Laughs*]: I've been through the wringer,
that's why I'm soft.

ANNA: I don't remember a time in my life
when I didn't feel hungry.
I counted every piece of bread.
All my life I've worried I might eat more than my share.
All my life I've been wearing rags.

SHLOMO: Poor woman.
You're worn out, that's all.

ANNA: I keep thinking,
O God,
am I to be punished in the next world too?

SHLOMO [*Stroking her forehead*]: No.
You'll have
a good rest up there.
You just need to bear up
a little longer,
then you'll have your rest.

How is your pulse?
Let me feel.

[*Holding her wrist, gently*]

A woman's pulse, you know, can be
sharp as a hook
or fine as a hair.
What do you think is normal?
How is your heart beating?
A pulse can be
like a string of pearls
like water dripping through the roof

like leaves scattering
like visiting strangers
like spring water welling up
like a smooth pill
like glory.

Your pulse is strong
and as smooth as a river.

ANNA: We really ought
to be better people, you know.
We're all the descendants of washerwomen.
This should have nurtured in us
some desire
to bring light
to the lives of our fellow beings
who have known nothing but
hardship
or hard work
all their lives.
Some of us were sent on ahead,
we were supposed to have the intelligence
to find a road to a better life.
And we've lost our way.

SHLOMO: There.
You've done all you could do.

ANNA: I'll go to hell for it.

SHLOMO: No.

ANNA: Yes, I will.

SHLOMO: We each do what we have within us to do
This is all we can do

[*While Shlomo talks, he returns to binding his book,
his practiced hands moving efficiently at the task;
we are transfixed by his hands;*

the room is absolutely quiet;
we watch him for a long while in silence.]

You might say
what I've done with my life
has been pointless.
It might be true.

[*Silence as he works*]

Possibly I should have done something else
[*Looks up, with a big smile*]
something that's not just
another of the pleasures for the few.

[*Silence*]

But I gave what I had
I couldn't give what I didn't have
so that
now
at the end
I might have to conclude
well:
it's been entirely meaningless
entirely meaningless,
and I'm too old now to start again.

[*Silence*]

Sometimes I cry myself to sleep.
And I'm a man.

[*Silence as we watch him work*]

ALEJANDRO: Let's play cards, shall we?
Tertius, will you play?

TERTIUS: Of course.

RAUL: I don't think you'll like our small stakes.

TERTIUS: It's not the stakes that matter.

[*We see* ALEJANDRO *at a rigged up table, shuffling a deck of cards* TERTIUS *joins him and* RAUL *and* KADIRA. *We see* BILLY *come back in from outdoors.*]

BILLY: Deal me in.

ALEJANDRO: The game is seven card stud. Ante ten cents.

[*Everyone puts in some coins.*]

KADIRA: I thought this was a friendly game.

ALEJANDRO: It *is* a friendly game.

KADIRA: Ante ten cents?

BILLY: I'll loan it to you.

KADIRA: That's all right.

BILLY: You can pay me back.

KADIRA: No. Thank you.

BILLY: Here. Take it.

[*The cards are dealt.*]

ALEJANDRO: This is the new capitalism, the thieves loaning money to the poor innocents of Eastern Europe.

RAUL [*While he looks at his cards*]: I don't understand it. I invest my whole life in a job, and I get just enough to get me to the next day

to do another day's work.
Why does someone think I don't have as much invested
as the owner?

BILLY: No. You don't understand it.

TERTIUS [*Idly, as he arranges his cards*]: Money is magic.
If you have money
you can move your factories to Mexico,
and then, when you take your profits
you can leave the polluted air behind you in Mexico,
and return to the clean air of Paris or London.
In this way, you can take a man's water,
a man's fresh air.
a man's suntan,
take years from his life
and add them to your own.
This is the true beauty of money.

ALEJANDRO: The stories people tell about business.
No one is ever interested.
But stories about love,
these are stories anyone can understand.

One night I remember
my lover came to me
to the arbor,

[RAUL *sneezes into his hand and says "bullshit,"
which stops Alejandro only momentarily.*]

as we had arranged.
I was already there waiting for him
trembling with grief and fear.
He, too, was trembling
his face as white as chalk
a revolver in his hand,
and he said to me in a deathly voice:
oh my dearest, my precious love,
my parents refuse to give their consent.

RAUL: His parents!

ALEJANDRO: And if we marry
they would disown me.

RAUL: What do his parents have to do with it?

SHLOMO: Sha. Quiet.

ALEJANDRO: And so I have no choice, he said, but to take my life.
I pleaded with him:
Oh, Marcel, I said . . .

RAUL: Marcel!
Last time it was Robert.

ALEJANDRO: What is the matter with you?
I'm telling you a love story.
Is it that you can't bear to hear it?

RAUL: I'm only saying
last time it was Robert.
So he's changed his name.
Or he had two names.

ALEJANDRO: I'm pouring my heart out to you,
I'm telling you about my life,
and what do you do?
You've become literary critics!
What do you know about love?

RAUL: We're just trying to understand what you say.

Maybe you've had many young men commit suicide for you.

SHLOMO: Okay, enough,
let her tell her story.

RAUL: Him.

SHLOMO: Him.

ALEJANDRO: Forget it.

SHLOMO: Go ahead.

ALEJANDRO: I can't tell the truth to these jerks;
they don't want to hear.
They're too afraid of emotions I think.
These men, you know how they are,
they'd rather talk business and politics.
What has business to do with you, you idiots?
Forget it!

RAUL: Go ahead.
Just try to keep your story straight.

ALEJANDRO: Oh!

RAUL: It's a good story
just very complicated.

SHLOMO: Let her tell it any way she wants!
It doesn't matter.
It's her story. His story.
This is how she feels.

JESSIE: Even if she read it from a book.

SHLOMO: Go on.

ALEJANDRO [*Near tears now*]: No, really.
Never mind.
It doesn't matter.
I couldn't tell anything now.
I'm too upset.

SHLOMO: Please.

[*Silence*]

ALEJANDRO: The magic word.

So I said to him:
oh, please, no.
My bright star.

[*Crying now, tears rolling down her cheeks*]

You musn't destroy your young life.
Forget me.
Forget me.
I'm not fit for anything.
But you have a life in front of you.
Leave me behind.
You go on, and live.
And know
I will always love you
as long as my heart beats in my breast.

[*Silence*]

BILLY: I recognize this;
it's from the book *Fatal Love*.

ALEJANDRO: It's from my life
you faggot.

BILLY: OK,
it's from your life.
It just sounded to me like *Fatal Love*.
But I've only read the jacket copy.

KADIRA: I think I've seen it on television.

ALEJANDRO: You don't have a television!

SHLOMO [*Putting an arm around Alejandro*]: Come along, dear.
Don't mind them.
I believe you.

ALEJANDRO: He was a Chilean boy,
a student.

SHLOMO: I believe it.
Come.

[*They go off to sit by Alejandro's bunk.*]

TERTIUS: When I was a young man
I was in love with a woman.
I saw her in the summer
at a picnic.
She was a married woman.
She had on a light summer dress
and as she walked toward me
the sun was behind her,
her dress was translucent,
she was wearing nothing underneath it.
Her eyes were sky blue,
sky blue.
I don't understand it:
people's passions are so unaccountable.
I fell in love with her,
so fragile she seemed.
I said to her:
we should have a summer love affair.
She didn't say no,
she said: you're outrageous.
I said: no, it's you who are outrageous.
We met the next day—
her husband stayed in the city all week to work,
and we made love every day the whole summer,
every day.

And still
I think of her
all the time.
Every day of my life.

KADIRA: I was once in love with a man.
I loved him so much
I would just put my arms around him
and then he would hold me,
he would hold me as gently as he could
and I would quiver
and come again and again,
and I would curl up inside his arms.
Whenever we made love, this is how we would always begin.
And every time after we made love
I would sob for a long time
with his arms around me.
Because,
I thought:
we might have lived our whole lives
and died
without ever knowing each other.

[*Silence.*

*The door to the landlord's apartment opens,
and Trang steps out onto the landing.*]

TRANG: Billy.

BILLY: Yes.

TRANG: Would you speak to me for a minute?

BILLY: Yes. Sure.
[*To his companions*]
I'm out.
[*He puts his cards down and goes to the stairs and up them.*]

RAUL: I win.

[*Billy is now with Trang on the landing.
They speak very quietly together.*]

TRANG: I thought you would want to see me.

BILLY: Want to see you?

TRANG: To say good morning.

BILLY: Oh.

TRANG: I speak to you from my heart
and fifteen minutes later
you can't remember when it was you last saw me.

BILLY: That's not true.

TRANG: It's true you don't care for me.

BILLY: Don't care for you . . .

TRANG: You know, you could just tell me.
You've fallen in love with someone else.

BILLY: Someone else?

TRANG: Look,
you think I know nothing.
I can tell when you have no connection to me.
It's okay.

BILLY: It's true I might have some conflicting feelings.
Maybe I shouldn't have,
I mean if I somehow let you believe that I . . .

TRANG: I counted on you to take me out of here with you.

BILLY: You did?
Did I know that?

TRANG: You don't want to leave?

BILLY: Well, yes, but . . .

TRANG: Anyhow, now I suppose that's not possible.

[*Silence*]

Now you love my sister.

BILLY [*Laughs*]: How do you know this?
I've hardly said two words to your sister.

[*Silence*]

TRANG: I could even help you, you know.

BILLY: How is that?

TRANG: I could give you money.

BILLY: What are you talking about?

TRANG: To go somewhere with her.

My husband is an old man,
I mean,
for his age
he hasn't taken care of himself.
If he were to fall
if something were to happen to him,
he is so delicate
I think it would kill him.

[*Silence*]

And then we'd be free of him,
and I could help you.

BILLY: I don't understand.

TRANG: Of course you do.
We've got a complication with him
as long as he's alive.

BILLY: You mean that I should kill your husband?

[*Silence*]

This is not the kind of person I am.

TRANG: How do you know?
Maybe you don't know what sort of person you are.

[*She turns and leaves.
He remains on the landing,
then turns slowly and walks down the stairs.*

*Nikos reels, falls against one of the bunks,
and starts collapsing to the floor.
Several of the others lunge to catch him from falling.*]

TERTIUS: Oh, steady on, I've got you.

ALEJANDRO: Here, I have him, too.

TERTIUS: Whoa, you've done a job of it this time.

SHLOMO: What's the matter with him?

TERTIUS: Heroin.

SHLOMO: Oh, no.
[*Talking now to Nikos, who is stretched out on his bunk*]
This is not a life for you.
You're a young man.
My God, this is no age to give up.
I've known men
who've had some trouble with drink or drugs.
They've gotten help;
you can get help yourself.
All you need is a few weeks in a hospital, you know.

TERTIUS: Shlomo.

SHLOMO: Yes?

TERTIUS: He doesn't understand a word you're saying.
He's Greek.

[*Silence.* SHLOMO *looks at Nikos, who gazes back at him.*]

SHLOMO: I think he does.

TERTIUS: No. Not a word.

[*Nikos slowly lies back in bed.
And, in the background, an argument erupts between Kadira and Jaroslaw.
Everyone turns in silence to take this in. It is a completely incomprehensible
argument to those of us who listen to it.*]

JAROSLAW: You say Turkic
but what do you know how it feels to be a Turk?

KADIRA: Let's say a person knows how it feels
to be conquered and forced to behave in a certain way.

JAROSLAW: So you feel bad
but this is not to feel Turkic!
You know, the Turks also formed empires.

KADIRA: I am talking about the Turkish military . . .

JAROSLAW: So am I.

KADIRA [*Exploding suddenly in uncontrolled and uncontrollable rage; yelling—
frightening*]: attacking its own citizens.

JAROSLAW: In Armenia the army is not used against its citizens.

KADIRA [*Still yelling*]: I didn't say it was.

JAROSLAW [*The words rolling out rapid fire*]: No. Exactly.
In Armenia a plane fires a rocket
that lands next to a woman holding the hand of her little daughter,
and the woman just disappears,
and the daughter's hand also disappears,

and she is crying "Mama, mama, mama"
with blood pouring from her arm,
running and running.

KADIRA [*Still in a rage*]: Yes.
Yes.
Or they rounded up two hundred women
took them to an empty slaughterhouse
made them strip naked
and get down on all fours
like cattle
they drove them forward
to a ramp
where they were

where the soldiers
lashed out at them
with knives
and axes
forcing them to

keep crawling
until they could crawl no more
their torsos
their arms and legs hacked off
their headless torsos
left to fall
into the pit below.

JAROSLAW: What is your point?

KADIRA: I am telling to you the truth!

JAROSLAW: For your information, the military is fighting the PKK, a terrorist
organization that even the Kurds despise.

KADIRA: Never mind.
I'm not talking to you.

JAROSLAW: I'm talking to you.

KADIRA: No. You are talking to yourself.

JAROSLAW: Nishto ne znaesh!

KADIRA: Iebise!

JAROSLAW: Ti se lebi!

[*At the end, no one has understood this any better than we have;
everyone is staring at Jaroslaw and Kadira in uncomprehending silence.*]

BILLY: What was that?

ALEJANDRO: Don't ask me.

BILLY: No, really, what was that all about?

RAUL: How the fuck should I know?

NGUYEN: There's water.

[*We see Nguyen standing on the landing, calling down.*]

Vinnie went out. I'm going to turn on the water!

[*Everyone starts hurriedly taking off their clothes,
down to their underclothes
and hurrying to one corner of the factory
where there is a thin partition
behind which is an overhead pipe
and a drain in the floor.*]

Okay. Two minutes.

[*The residents of the factory strip—
one or two of them keep on their clothes—
and step under the stream of water from the pipe.*

*And they each take a shower
in what must be reminiscent of a prison scene.*

Our gaze lingers on each one, stripped naked;
there is no prurient interest here,
just an interest in human individuality,
and in sagging, out-of-shape human flesh.
There should be something of sadness about this.

Those standing in line are patient for a few moments
as they wait for each person who steps into the shower,
and then they begin to say things like "Hurry up . . . move along . . . that's all . . .
    don't use up all the water. . . .etc. in a constant chatter.

BILLY, *meanwhile, walks up the stairs to follow Nguyen back into the landlord's*
    house.

Just as he reaches the top of the stairs, he looks back down, and we see that the
    water has just run out, before the last two people in line could have a
    shower—and they are complaining.]

JAROSLAW: Come on. Come on.
How can you be so slow?
Do you think everyone doesn't want a turn?

NGUYEN [*To Billy*]: What are you doing?

BILLY: I've got something for you.

NGUYEN: What?

BILLY: Your papers, from Vinnie's safe.

NGUYEN: You've stolen them?

BILLY: Yes.

NGUYEN: Why?

[*Silence*]

So that I belong to you?

BILLY: I hadn't thought of that.

NGUYEN: No?

BILLY: No.
Well, maybe for a moment.
But I've dropped it.

[*He gives the papers to her.*]

NGUYEN: You're just going to give them to me?

BILLY: Yeah.

NGUYEN: For nothing?

BILLY: Yeah.
For nothing.

[*She takes his face in her hands and kisses him.*
He hesitates, then kisses her back.
She kisses him back.
They kiss each other passionately.]

BILLY: Only one thing:
when Vinnie discovers your papers are gone from the safe
he's going to guess you have them.

NGUYEN: Sure, I know.

BILLY: So there is a time limit,
how much longer you can stay.

NGUYEN: I wish I could be with you all the time.

BILLY: So do I.

[*Silence*]

NGUYEN: Will you leave with me?

BILLY: Yes.

NGUYEN: Tonight?

BILLY: Yes.

[*She turns quickly and goes back into the house.
Meanwhile the showering has ended
and party preparations begin.*]

TERTIUS: Here, Billy, you can give me a hand.

BILLY: Are these the glasses for champagne?

TERTIUS: Yes.

[*Each with a dish towel, they meticulously clean an assortment of glasses, mugs,
cans, jelly jars, etc. to use as glasses. We watch them clean every speck off each
container, while, in the background, the others set out food.*

*Meanwhile we see the bottles of champagne chilling in the pots and buckets used
to catch dripping water.*]

BILLY: I'll be getting out of here soon, you know.

TERTIUS: I didn't know.

BILLY: Every night as I go to sleep
I nearly choke.

TERTIUS: I think there are things that everyone feels
at least once every fifteen minutes for no reason at all:
a flood of grief, or dread, or hatred, a tinge of regret,
an unreasoning rage.
These are all things that come over me,
and I find I am powerless to resist them.
So I try just to accept
whatever sensations life sends my way.

[*They finish with the glasses, and Tertius opens a bottle of champagne.*]

Ladies and gentlemen, let me give you some champagne.

JAROSLAW: Is this champagne stolen?

TERTIUS: Stolen first from the bosom of the earth
and then from the capitalist bastards who stole it.

JAROSLAW: I have a problem drinking stolen champagne.

TERTIUS: Ah, well,
de gustibus non disputandem est.
Jessie?

JESSIE: I don't have a problem.
I put my faith in capitalism.
[*She offers a glass to Tertius for him to pour her a drink.*]

TERTIUS: Good.
Every experience of life
is an experience of being alive.
[*Pouring a glass for her*]

RAUL: Goddam you, you fucking cocksucker
[*We see him banging his shoe repeatedly, violently on the floor.*]
goddam you to fucking hell goddammit

BILLY: What is it, Raul?

RAUL [*Close to tears*]
This goddam fucking shoe won't go on my fucking foot.

BILLY: It's okay.

KADIRA: I'll help you.

[*She takes the shoe from him and starts to put it on his foot.*]

TERTIUS: Have some champagne.

[*He gives a glass to Raul.*]

This is not, I think,
an entirely despicable vintage,

[*As he pours glasses and hands them to the guests, he speaks.*]

and, to be sure,
whatever its provenance and pedigree,
whatever unique qualities it possesses,
champagne is an event—
one of the finest achievements of our civilization,
an exquisite product of human intelligence
of forethought and patience,
of the accumulated knowledge of cultivation and care,
the subtle, intricate cooperation
between nature and human beings
of the qualities of the earth itself,
of the soil, the air, the sun—
so that we drink not only with champagne but also,
at the same time: *to* it,
and to the complexity and beauty of life itself
and, finally, to all those things we love best.

ALEJANDRO: Well, then,
I drink to T-shirts from Liquid Sky
a how-to course for walking in stilettos
Dom Casual's pink, terry panties with a silk crotch
And lemon body mist.

SHLOMO: To a wool cardigan sweater
not a new cardigan, but an old cardigan
of dark green wool
to a first edition of Diderot's encyclopedia
signed if possible
a small house in Normandy with a little kitchen garden
a set of copper pots and pans
an old woman
one, if possible,
to whom I have been married for thirty years
three children
no longer living at home

to some geese
and a dog.

JAROSLAW: To an afternoon nap

ANNA: to sheets and pillowcases
white cotton or muslin

TERTIUS: To moss

ALEJANDRO: Yes. Indeed.
Or a fresh pomegranate

TERTIUS: A pear tree.

ANNA: The earth itself.

SHLOMO: Dirt.

SEVERAL: To dirt.
Dirt.

ANNA: The sunlight you see in water
as you pour it from a pitcher into a bowl.

[*Silence*]

I would like to live in a large, beautiful house. My family would stay with me,
and in one of the wings I would have a friend, a woman friend. And whenever
we wished, we would meet to discuss recent poems and other things of interest. When my friend received a letter, we would read it together and write our
answer. If someone came to pay my friend a visit, I would receive him in one
of our beautifully decorated rooms, and if he were prevented from leaving by
a rain-storm or something of the sort, I would invite him to stay.

ALEJANDRO: But why do you think it is that boys like fresh lemon body mist?
And why do they always want you to make love in a public place?
Or want you to wear a rubber dress that makes a squeaky sound when you
    put it on?

JESSIE: This is how men are.

ALEJANDRO: There are men who simply won't look twice
unless you're wearing rubber stockings
or rubber pants
rubber gloves
or some body jewelry
a leather bracelet, or a collar
or something that has a battery attached to it
a little bit of piercing somewhere.

JAROSLAW: Of course, you all want these things given to you
These are things other people work for.

RAUL: Or take from someone else.

JAROSLAW: Oh, yes, these poor bastards
always having everything taken from them.
It's a lie!
You don't have anything to take!

RAUL: We don't?

JAROSLAW: No!

RAUL: We don't?

JAROSLAW: Nothing anyone wants.

RAUL: Not oil?

JAROSLAW: This is not yours!
This is in the ground!
You don't get it out!
The Americans get it out!
They come in with their know-how and they get it out!
You don't lift a goddam finger,
and yet you get paid for it.
You get paid for it.

RAUL: It belongs to us, you fucking nutcase.
And we get it out.
This is our labor you pay for.

JAROSLAW: Your labor!
You lazy bastards
you lie about all day
and then complain about your wages!
It's not fair, you say,
it's not fair, it's not fair.
I tell you: I put my faith in capitalism!

RAUL: You'll be surprised
when someone puts a fucking suitcase bomb in your subway.

KADIRA: His subway?
This Polack?

JAROSLAW: Now you think I should be afraid of a war with you—
you people don't know how to get a plane off the ground.

KADIRA: You think I am an Iraqi?
You think I am an Iraqi?
You don't even know who I am!
You people sit there
have the Russians and the Germans run back and forth
back and forth
back and forth
up and down your backsides
and you tell me I don't know how to fight?

So OK.
OK.
Never mind.
In fact, one day soon this evil system will defeat itself.

JAROSLAW: This is garbage.

KADIRA: What is?

JAROSLAW: What you say,
everything you say.

KADIRA: This is my religion.

JAROSLAW: Your religion is garbage.

KADIRA [*Sudden uncontrolled rage; yelling*]: You know, I could cut your
    fucking throat.

JAROSLAW [*Contemptuously*]: With what?

KADIRA [*Taking a butcher knife from the table*]: With this, you asshole!

[JESSIE *and* BILLY *step forward instantly,*
with the instincts of people who have often been in the midst
of sudden violence, holding both Jaroslaw and Kadira back.]

TERTIUS [*Stepping between them*]: Ah, ah, ah, ah, I'll be needing that to cut
    the cake.

KADIRA [*Still yelling*]: You should be nice to me.
I haven't done you any wrong.

JAROSLAW: If you knew how to do *anything*
it would be wrong.

KADIRA: What do you mean, you sonofabitch?

[*Kadira breaks free and shoves Jaroslaw violently;*
JAROSLAW *falls backward,*
crashing through Jessie's cart full of stuff,
scattering it,
landing heavily on the floor]

SHLOMO [*Quietly, sadly*]: Oh, no.

BILLY: Here. That's enough.

[*Billy and several others help Jaroslaw to his feet
while Jessie and others restrain Kadira.*]

BILLY [*Helping Jaroslaw*]: Are you all right?

JAROSLAW [*To Raul*]: I'll rip your goddam arms off!

SHLOMO: Here. Settle down now.

JAROSLAW: Let go of me.

KADIRA: I'll rip *your* fucking arms off.

[*The fight subsides.*]

ALEJANDRO: Do you wear rubber?

KADIRA: Rubber?

ALEJANDRO: You know, rubber, like rubber skirts, or, in the summer, rubber
    shorts or rubber stockings, or even—you know, rubber underwear.

KADIRA: No.

ALEJANDRO: I thought you might.

[*Silence*]

Most people, you know, try to repair their rubber with Superglue, which is
    fatal, because it destroys the material.

KADIRA: No, I didn't know.

ALEJANDRO: I use Copydex for temporary repairs,
but then I always take it into a professional.

KADIRA: What are you telling me?

ALEJANDRO: I just thought you might like to know.
You never can tell when it might be useful.

You know, to get leather or rubber on, you have to make sure you're dry from
head to toe, and then talc yourself.

SHLOMO: Life is more complicated now than it used to be.

TERTIUS: Of course there used to be rules.

JAROSLAW: There are now.

ALEJANDRO: Oh, sure. But now everyone knows they're just made up.
Like the rules for
the Honey Bee or the Cart Wheel
or the Lovely Lady in Control
or the Coitus of the Gods.

JESSIE: The Coitus of the Gods?

JAROSLAW: Now we have to listen to more filth.

JESSIE: I'd like to hear.

ALEJANDRO: You hold each other's hands,
sprawled like two starfish making love,
her thighs stretched out along yours,
and you hold each other for a long, long time: that's all.

[*Silence as everyone thinks about this.*]

TERTIUS: Ah, but I'd almost forgotten:
there is entertainment this evening.
I have arranged for one of the great classical actors of our time
to render for us
some passages from the immortal comic genius of antiquity,
the playwright Aristophanes.
Here,
from Aristophanes' great work *The Birds:*

[NIKOS *nods, takes a moment to prepare,*
and then launches into his performance—
complete with bird impersonations,

flapping and leaping up and down like a bird,
and so forth.
(Once again, only the Greek is delivered; the English translation here is just for
the convenience of the actor.)]

NIKOS: hos d' ouchi theori toninun erchon ton anthropon to palaion,
all' ornithes, kabasileuon, poll'esti tekmeria touton.
Aiguptou d' au kai Phoinikes pases kokkux basileus en:
chopoth' ho kokkuk eipoi "kokku' tot" an hoi Phoinikes
hapantes tous purous an kai tas krithas en tois pediois etherizon.
erchon d' houto sphodra ten archen,
host ei tis kai basileuoi en tais polesin ton Hellenon Agamemnon e Menelaos,
epi ton skeptron ekathet ornis metechon ho ti dorokokoie.
ho de deinotaton g estin hapanton,
ho Zeus gar ho nun basileuon aieton ornin hesteken echon epi tes kephales
        basileus on,
he d' au thugater glauch',
ho d' Apollon hosper therapon hieraka.

[It was not the gods, but the birds,
who were formerly the masters and kings over men;
of this I have a thousand proofs.
The cuckoo was the king of Egypt and of the whole of Phoenicia.
When he called out "cuckoo,"
all the Phoenicians hurried to the fields to reap their wheat and their barley.
So powerful were the birds that the kings of Grecian cities, Agamemnon,
Menelaus,
for instance, carried a bird on the tip of their scepters, who had his share of
all presents.
But the strongest proof of all is that Zeus, who now reigns,
is represented as standing with an eagle on his head as a symbol of his royalty;
his daughter has an owl,
and Phoebus, as his servant, has a hawk.]

[TERTIUS *applauds*
shouts bravo—
speaks a few words of Greek
to encourage Nikos to take repeated bows.
Everyone else remains completely unmoved and silent.
BILLY, *out of embarrassment and compassion for Nikos*

applauds a few times.
Then there is awkward silence.]

SHLOMO [*To save embarrassment*]: If this is the proper moment, then,
I'd like to sing a song
that we used to sing in my home when I was a child.

TERTIUS: Please.

SHLOMO: Luz mir alle inanem inanem
[name of person] makable punim zein
Luz mir alle inanem inanem
[name of person] makable punim zein
Luz mir alle namem
Luz mir alle namem
Trinken ah glazelah v-i-n-e.
Luz mir alle namem
Luz mir alle namem
Trinken ah glazelah v-i-n-e.

[*The song repeats, adding others' names in as it goes along.*

Alejandro joins in dancing with him;
this moment is prolonged;
Shlomo and Alejandro enjoy dancing with each other;
then Kadira, then others join in.

On the end of Shlomo's song,
Jaroslaw begins his own song and dance
that the others also join in as they get the hang of it.]

JAROSLAW: Ya kazhi mi, oblache le, byalo
of gde idesh, gde si mi letyalo
Ne vidya li bashtini mi dvori
I ne chu li maika da govori.?
Shto li pravi moito chedo milo,
s chuzhdi hora, chuzhdi hlyab delilo?
Ti kazhi I, olbache le, byalo,
zhiv I zdrav, che tuk si me vidyalo.
I nosi of mene mnogo zdrave,

mnogo mina, munichko ostana.
Nablizhava v selo da se vurna
da se vurna, maika da pregurna.

[Tell me, little white cloud,
Where are you coming from, where have you flown.
Did you see my father's home
and did you hear my mother talk?
How is my precious child doing,
sharing foreign bread with foreign people?
You tell her, little white cloud,
that you saw me here, strong and healthy,
and send my love to her,
a lot of time has passed, and not much is left.
It's fine for me to go back,
to go back and give my mother a hug.]

VINNIE PAZZI [*From the top of the landing as he starts to rush down the stairs*]:
What are you doing, you bastards,
burning down the house?

[*Silence*]

Smoke is pouring up the stairs
and you're dancing!

What's the matter with you?

You didn't hear what I said?

Put this out!
Put this out!

[*He grabs a bucket of water, sending a champagne bottle smashing on the floor, and dumps it onto the barbecue grill; he kicks the grill over onto the floor, gets another bucket and dumps the water onto the scattered food and hot charcoal.*]

Cooking over an open fire:
this is for barbarians!

BILLY [*Taking a firm hold on Vinnie Pazzi, speaking quietly*]: Stop.

VINNIE PAZZI: Don't touch me, you prick.

BILLY: You'll be lucky if I don't break your neck.

VINNIE PAZZI: Are you threatening me?
Do you hear this?
He threatens me in my own house.
I could throw you out of here any moment I want.

BILLY: You throw me out, I'll have you put in jail.

VINNIE PAZZI: For what?

BILLY: For receiving stolen goods!
For selling stolen goods!

VINNIE PAZZI: You can't prove a thing.

BILLY: I have people who will testify against you.

VINNIE PAZZI: Oh, do you?
Who is that?
Who?

TERTIUS [*With Raul helping him pull Billy and Vinnie Pazzi apart*]:
That's enough now.
Come.

BILLY: People from your own house.

VINNIE PAZZI: From my house!

TERTIUS: That's all.

JAROSLAW [*Shouting*]: Have you no respect for the dead?

BILLY: What?

[*Silence as all turn to Jaroslaw
who is in complete anguish and despair,
tears pouring down his face,
holding Anna in his arms*]

JAROSLAW: Can't you see that my wife has died?
[*Holding her*]
Oh, Anna.
Anna.
Anna.

[SHLOMO *puts his arm around Jaroslaw.*]

SHLOMO: There, there,
she's at peace now.

VINNIE PAZZI: She's died here in my house?
Goddammit,
now what do you think
what kind of bullshit am I going to have now
with the county health department?
Goddammit,
no one told me she was that sick,
and you let her stay here when she could die on my premises?
You bastards!

[*He starts for the stairway.*]

I'll phone the coroner's office.
You get her out of here into the alley,
I'm not having any trouble over this.

[*Shouting ahead as he goes up the stairs*]

Trang! Nguyen!
Call the coroner's office.
Someone's died
goddammit.

SHLOMO: Come.
Bring a sheet for her.
Here, Jaroslaw, just let go for a moment now,
sit just here close to her
but let me cover her.

[*Jaroslaw, still crying,*
slowly surrenders her body to Shlomo.
Others come with a sheet
and help to wrap Anna in it.
Still others come to Jaroslaw and hug him.]

NGUYEN [*From atop the landing*]: I've called an undertaker and the police.

BILLY: The police?

NGUYEN: Yes.

SHLOMO: Why the police?

NGUYEN: I shouldn't have called the police?

BILLY: It's nothing to do with the police.
That's all right, it doesn't matter.

TERTIUS: Here, give me a hand.

[*All the men are picking up Anna to carry her upstairs.*
She is shrouded in a sheet.
They all carry her, with Jaroslaw following behind,
and then the others behind him.
Talk of "okay," "here, I have her" etc. as they go upstairs.
On the landing there is now a huge crowd
and a lot of maneuvering to get through the door
into the landlord's house.
Just inside the door, VINNIE PAZZI *meets them.*]

VINNIE PAZZI [*Enraged*]: What are you doing
bringing her in here?

RAUL: You said to take her outside.

VINNIE PAZZI: To the alley, you schmuck,
not through my house.
What are you doing bringing a dead body into my house?

BILLY: Just have some compassion for . . .

VINNIE PAZZI: Just get this corpse out of my house, goddammit,
you let them in here?

NGUYEN: I . . .

VINNIE PAZZI: You opened the door to this mob?

NGUYEN: I . . .

[*Vinnie Pazzi slaps her.*]

VINNIE PAZZI: You stupid bitch!

BILLY: What happened?

TERTIUS: That was uncalled for, I think.

VINNIE PAZZI: What do you know?

[*He snatches up a tea pot and throws it at Nguyen,
who shrieks in pain.*]

BILLY: That's all.

[*There is now an explosion of frightening violence.*

Billy shoves his way through the crowd toward Vinnie Pazzi.
The others are all struggling to get to him, too.
The class war begins.
Someone shoves Vinnie Pazzi,
Vinnie Pazzi spins around off balance
into the crowd of pallbearers,

and now Billy grabs him by the shoulders
and propels him back out through the door
onto the landing
where he gives him a tremendous shove
—and, as Billy then turns to run to Nguyen,
we hear Vinnie Pazzi scream out, and then,
as Billy pulls Nguyen into his arms,
we hear another scream from one of the women
then more shouting
and finally Tertius, who happens to be near Billy speaks.]

TERTIUS: He has fallen over the railing.

BILLY: What?

TERTIUS: Your landlord has fallen over the railing
into the factory.

[*Stunned silence.*

The crowd is ashen-faced
at the instant realization of what they have done.

BILLY *gets up*
moves through the crowd of his companions
to look over the railing.
Already some of the others are running down the stairs.
Billy runs after them.
They part to let him to Vinnie Pazzi's side.
Billy looks at him,
reaches out to touch him,
pulls back an eyelid,
puts his head to Vinnie Pazzi's chest to listen for a heartbeat.
Billy is stunned.]

BILLY [*Under his breath*]: I've killed him.

RAUL: The police are here.

[BILLY *looks up to see the police coming down the stairs.*]

POLICEMAN: Well, what have we here?
Is he hurt?

BILLY: He's dead.

POLICEMAN: Dead?

[*The policeman kneels down to examine Vinnie Pazzi,
confirms he is dead.*]

Was he a friend of yours?

BILLY: No.

POLICEMAN: How did it happen?

TRANG: He pushed him.

POLICEMAN: Who?

TRANG: That man,
he pushed my husband over the railing and killed him.

POLICEMAN: Did you?

[*Silence.
Kadira steps forward.*]

KADIRA: I'm the one who pushed him.
He pushed me.
So I pushed him back.

RAUL: Oh, well, I pushed him.

ALEJANDRO: Well, really, I think I'm the one who pushed him.

RAUL: I think we were all pushing each other.

TERTIUS: Excuse me, officer.
Tertius Hodgson.

POLICEMAN: Yes?

TERTIUS: If I can be of any assistance.
I saw the entire incident.

POLICEMAN: And?

TERTIUS: It was an accident.
A woman died here today,
and these gentlemen were carrying the body of this poor man's wife
up through the house
to take her for burial.
There was so little room on the staircase
and such a crowd of people,
I think everyone was jostling
don't you know
and under such stress in any case.
This unfortunate fellow lost his balance.
I think he had been a bit confused for some years in any case,
if you know what I mean.
And, in any event, he fell over the railing.
It's a tragedy.
I don't think anyone's to be blamed.

POLICEMAN: That's your story.

[*Silence as he looks around from one person to another.*]

That's your story.

TERTIUS: If there are further inquiries
you can ask for me here.

POLICEMAN: Thank you.

[*To Trang*]

If I could speak to you for a moment upstairs.

TRANG: Yes.

POLICEMAN [*To Billy*]: And you,
don't leave.
There may be further questions for you.

[*The policeman starts out upstairs;
Tertius gently takes Trang's arm.*]

TERTIUS: I hope you don't mind my speaking up to the officer.
You know,
in this country,
the courts can be so difficult
sorting out any questions of inheritance
if there is some question of foul play.
I thought you would want to be spared all that.
If you're to be our landlady now,
you'll have enough on your mind without that sort of trouble.

[*She turns to follow the policeman upstairs.*]

TERTIUS [*To Nguyen*]: Will you have some champagne?
Life is such a mixed bag,
hardly ever all good or all bad.

[*He gives her a glass of champagne and has one himself;
it is dark now in the factory;
the light bulbs in the green conical shades are lit.*]

Where is Shlomo?

RAUL: He's disappeared.

ALEJANDRO: He got his things and left
the moment Nguyen said she had called the police.

TERTIUS: Really?

KADIRA: What did he have to hide?

RAUL: I'd go myself if there were someplace to go.

TERTIUS: If you have no connections to hold you here, why not?

JESSIE: If it weren't for my feet, I'd hit the road myself.

RAUL: I'd go, but I just got here.
I meant to go somewhere.
I mean: I thought I did go somewhere,
but as it turned out
I just came here.

KADIRA: I'd like to go.

BILLY: If it hadn't been for the cop telling me to stay,
we'd have been leaving.

TERTIUS: We?

BILLY: Nguyen and I.

RAUL: Leaving here?

TERTIUS: Do you mean now?

BILLY: Yes.

[*Surprise, silence*]

NGUYEN: Well, you can come upstairs with me
and stay there until we leave.

BILLY: Upstairs?

NGUYEN: It's as much mine
as my sister's.

[*All turn to look at Billy,
their new landlord.*]

KADIRA: Well, this is how it is:
every man for himself, eh?
We live in a world where the thieves rise to the top.

[*Silence*]

ALEJANDRO: Or you could say: where love is still possible.

KADIRA: Yes, well, I put my faith in capitalism for sure.

[*She turns and walks away.*

Silence.

Tertius steps forward,
embraces Billy.]

TERTIUS: I wish you well.
You made me feel at home here when I first arrived.
I wish you both the very best.

[*Silence again;*
finally RAUL *steps forward.*]

JESSIE: I say good luck to both of you.

[*Everyone gathers to shake hands,*
hug Nguyen, say goodbye—
only Kadira standing aloof.]

RAUL: I for one,
I'd be in your place if I could be.

ALEJANDRO: Well,
you must have us to dinner when you've settled in your new home.

[*After a moment, Billy and Nguyen turn away*
and go to Billy's shelves,
take stuff from the shelves and toss them in a duffle bag.
Awkward silence.]

TERTIUS: It is so hard for me to understand the customs here.
Two people have died,
and no one mourns.

Is this how it is?

[*In response to this remark,
Jessie sings a soulful, melancholy solo—
a blues song or hymn—
that turns in the end into a positive song.*]

THE END